The Smell of Lilacs
A Memoir

Michal Ramsey Smith

The Smell of Lilacs: a memoir

For more information about this title or to order other books
and/or electronic media, contact the publisher:

Atkins & Greenspan Publishing
18530 Mack Avenue, Suite 166
Grosse Pointe Farms, MI 48236
TwoSistersWriting.com

ISBN:
978-1-956879-06-3 (Paperback)
978-1-956879-07-0 (eBook)

Printed in the United States of America

All the stories in this work are true.

Cover and Graphic Design: Van-garde Imagery, Inc.
Photo credit for author photo: Ashleigh Spann
Kitchen photo sketch: Artist Kristin Prosser

Dedication

For Ashleigh Zannett

You have the style of your Great-Great Aunt Laura and weep often as did your Great Aunt Marie. Much like your Great-Great Aunt Sylvinie, you don't miss much, and you are a fabulous cook, your specialty a spaghetti that would make Cousin Martha proud. And, you carry the name of your Grandmother Zannett into the next generation.

I love you, daughter of mine.

And for Rocky.

My past,

My present,

My future,

My always.

Contents

Introduction

This is a story about my family. There are things about the people in this story that I don't know. There are things I do know that you don't need to know.

The whole thing started many years ago when, as a teacher for the Saginaw Public Schools, I attended an after-school workshop. I don't recall what the workshop was all about or the name of the person who conducted it. We were asked to write a descriptive paragraph of 25 to 50 words. Grudgingly, I did so. Mine described my Aunt Marie. I quickly scribbled it out, was relieved when I didn't have to share with the group, balled up the sheet, and dropped it into the wastebasket on my way out.

But I found myself, over time, thinking about her and the other women and men in my family—wonderful people who encircled me in their cloak of love and laughter, dignity and respect—and slowly the writing took life. I chose to write this story looking through a narrow lens, the summers and falls in 1956 and 1958.

Do not for a moment believe that I believe that the people here were perfect without flaws and faults. They weren't. But they loved me, and I loved them, and that to me is power that must be shared and passed on.

Artist: Kristin Prosser

The Beginning

I stood at my kitchen stove, carefully turning over pieces of chicken as they sizzled and browned in the large cast iron skillet. Collard greens, seasoned with ham hocks, simmered gently on the back burner. The sweet sugary aroma of plain cake wafted from the oven, filling the air. Twelve ears of corn shucked the night before sat on the counter, ready to be cut from the cob for frying.

Preparations were underway for Sunday dinner. The family was coming, my brothers, nephews and their children, my daughter. The past year had been a difficult one for us. There had been illness and loss when we banded together to give solace, hope, and comfort. This gathering, however, was a "just because" time. Just because we could and would be together. There would be lots of laughter, happy hugs, and fabulous food. The last not a modest thing to say, but the truth nonetheless.

I loved to cook, did much of my serious thinking and problem solving during the making of sauces, stews, pies, and cakes. I found myself reflecting this Sunday morning as I moved around my small cozy kitchen space on things past: other places, other people, other events. I recalled other gatherings from the summer of 1956 when my family would come together to celebrate my sister's arrival, to *ooh* and *ahh* over the six-pound, twelve-ounce bundle that was the last born of the five children of my parents, Charles Otis and Zannett Clopton Ramsey. Leaning against the sink, I closed my eyes and opened my mind, letting the memories come... and I was home again.

Part One

Zannett: Part 1

She swung her legs over the side of the big four poster bed, carefully slid her feet into white Daniel Green mules, stood, and took the first steps of Saturday. From a hook on the door of the small bedroom closet to the left of the bed, she took a floor-length robe, known as a duster, and slipped it over the pale blue sleeveless shortie gown. She had several dusters, all similar: pale blue or pink, strewn with tiny flowers, small, rounded collars edged in white lace, eight tiny tan buttons tiptoeing down its front. There was always a string of safety pins attached to the left side of the robe. Sometimes there were two or three, other times 10 or 12; you always knew where to find one.

She would often put the duster on inside out, or with part of the collar turned up and part turned down. It didn't matter. Whichever way my mother, Zannett Clopton Ramsey, put it on… that was how it stayed. Most times, she wore this outfit for the entire day, too busy with the duties of the day to think about either primping or changing, but this was Saturday, and there was shopping to do.

In our house on the corner of Second and Johnson Streets in Saginaw, Michigan, Saturday always felt like the beginning of the week. It was the day shopping was done, preparations for Sunday dinner were made, and baths were grudgingly taken.

My mother went through the living and dining rooms, into the big kitchen at the back of the house, and got the coffee started. After filling the six-cup percolator with cold water, three scoops of ground Maxwell House coffee were added to the basket, the top replaced, the pot set on the back burner of the gas stove, and the fire turned to medium-high. She waited until the water heated, bubbled up, and began the gentle *plup, plup, plup* of percolation before turning the burner down until it clicked into place at the lowest setting.

The statement, "turn it to a click," was standard Ramsey language in our household for "heat the coffee," something my older brother, Lester Stewart, and I did throughout the day.

Our mother started breakfast for my father, who would be up and dressed for work shortly. Thick slices of slab bacon, two fried eggs, grits, toast, coffee, and a three-ounce glass of canned grapefruit juice.

Upstairs, the house remained quiet. There were three bedrooms. At the top of the stairs on the left, across from the bathroom, was a large bedroom, shared by my younger brothers, Ronald Otis and Douglas Wayne, who at three had graduated from crib to big boy bed. Down the hall from the bathroom was my small bedroom, and at the end of the hallway, the largest bedroom was the domain of my big brother Lester. Always an early riser, I waited at the top of the stairs for Mama to come up to the bathroom.

Always the same question.

"Good morning, Macki, did you wash your face and brush your teeth?"

Always the same reply.

"Yes, Ma'am, good morning."

In the kitchen, my father finished his breakfast.

My daddy, Charles Otis Ramsey, was a good-lookin' man. Tall, straight and muscular, he was chocolate, the semi-sweet kind—words one could use to describe both his skin color and personality. His steel grey hair was close-cropped, his smooth velvety face clean-shaven. He had big hands, bad feet and brittle bones, having broken both ankles, a wrist, and an elbow playing baseball in his youth. He always wore stiffly starched white shirts and dark suits. When he got to work at Cantu's Barber Shop on Third and Potter, he traded the suit jacket for a white barber's coat.

At the kitchen table, Daddy took out the big black billfold that was attached to his belt with a silver link chain. Holding it close to his chest, he would peer inside, looking as though he expected that things in the wallet had changed. Carefully, he extracted one ten- and one five-dollar bill and laid each beside his empty plate. Grocery money.

Mama returned to the kitchen and she and Daddy spoke softly for a few moments before he left by the back door, got into our three-year-old, powder blue 1953 Oldsmobile 98, and drove the eight blocks to the barber shop.

Daddy's departure meant that there would be about 20 minutes before Mama and I would leave to go to town shopping, so I dressed, fixed and ate a bowl of cornflakes in the kitchen, and waited.

I have often been told that I look like my mother. I didn't really think so, but if it were true, I took it as a great compliment, because in my eyes, she was incredibly beautiful. In contrast to my father, Zannett was small and petite, five-foot-three, perhaps 120 pounds. Dark brown eyes, set in a surprisingly large, round freckled face, gave her a look of perpetual calm that I am sure she did not always feel. She wore bright blood-red colored lipstick, and nail polish that matched, a surprising choice for someone so fair, and first impressions were often that she was Hispanic.

The child of a white father and Creole mother, she was cream with a drop of chicory-flavored coffee. She had "good hair," jet-black and straight. She shampooed with Castille soap, rinsed with vinegar, and when it was wet, she pressed a pencil down the sides of her hair to create waves. Sometimes shoulder-length, but most often cut short by my father, her hair was always parted on the right, and in her 62 years of life, it never grayed.

She told me once that when she was a child in Louisiana, she begged her grandmother to "press" her hair with a hot comb like all the other kids. When her grandmother finally obliged, the heat burned a big chunk of hair, which promptly fell out.

As an adult, my mother did not drink alcohol, preferring the caffeine kick of small bottles of Coca-Cola. She never swore, not even the word "butt." She was soft-spoken, rarely raising her voice. With her children, volume was not necessary. She could call your name in a certain tone while looking you "dead in the eyes" and you confessed, hung your head, and promised to do better next time. You knew from her voice when she was tickled, tired, angry, or disappointed. Like my brothers and sister, I really hated to detect disappointed.

For our shopping trip, my mother was dressed in a black skirt, topped with an orange and white, vertically-striped, sleeveless, loose-fitting blouse. The top covered the bump which was my sister, who would soon make her arrival—the fifth and final.

Downtown Saginaw was the same as small town downtowns across America: a busy bustling place in a time before malls and mega-stores made their appearance. Shops and stores lined both sides of Genesee Street from Weadock to Washington. Each cross street—Warren, Jefferson, Franklin, Baum—branching left and right, housed smaller shops, the post office, library, and two movie theaters. We would be making two stops for sure, Home Dairy Foods and Baisley's Meat Market. Our house was five blocks from downtown. Two blocks down Johnson Street, past Butz Grocery Store and the Merret Meat Packing Co., a left turn onto Warren for the three-block walk to Genesee Street, and we were in the heart of Saginaw's downtown.

In 1956, we didn't have Walmart; we had Home Dairy, and in that world, that store had everything: canned and packaged foods, fresh produce, a bakery, and a lunch counter. Mama and I had done this so often that no words were needed. I went to the lunch counter, climbing up onto the dark green stool. My feet dangled, not touching the floor. The lady behind the counter handed me a warm glazed donut, and I sat savoring each sugary, gooey bite while my mother shopped. She kept me in her sights as she moved around the store, and when her purchases were made and packed into brown shopping bags, she beckoned. I slid off the stool and we left, walking two doors down to the meat market.

A long narrow building, Baisley's was painted bright white with a black and white checked linoleum floor. White meat coolers lined down the left side, shoulder to shoulder, soldiers waiting for their orders. Beef, pork, chicken, lamb, and veal filled the cases, their deep reds and pinks a stark contrast to the pale white coated butchers who took orders and wrapped your choices in white paper, secured with white string. The butcher gave my mother a white bill of due, which she took to the glass booth on the right side of the store. Payment made, the white packages—hamburger, sausage, round steak, pork chops, and neck bones—were loaded into a brown shopping bag.

Downtown shopping was always a social occasion. We saw friends and acquaintances from the neighborhood, church, and school. My mother was well-known and well-liked, and she stopped often on our Saturday journey to greet, gab, and share local gossip. Each time Mama stopped, I stood by silently, smiling politely. This was adult conversation, and I knew well the rules: children did not comment, did not correct, DID NOT interrupt.

By the time we got home, my 13-year-old brother Les was ready to make the trip to Weir's Poultry for three fresh chickens. This was a nasty, messy job that he so hated. Purchased live, the chickens were dressed, double wrapped in white butcher paper and put in a paper bag, but the package always leaked, and by the time Les got it home, it was a bloody mess. Once home, my brother dumped the bloody birds into the kitchen sink and made his escape outside and around the corner to hang out with friends.

For me, the absolute best place in the entire world was beside my mother at the kitchen sink. Sometimes on a chair, often on tiptoe, talking softly to my Mama, while we worked on preparations for the Sunday family meal. Age and use had turned the once white sink a dull, almost sepia, tone and no amount of Comet Cleanser was going to make it not so. The hot and cold faucets were reversed, the result of one of my father's Sunday afternoon plumbing adventures. To the left of the sink, the counter was ridged, meant to be used for drainage. Instead, it was home to the big black-brown knobbed radio that played softly from early morning to late night. On the right side of the sink, a dish drainer sat, almost always cuddling spoons, plates, cups, saucers, and bowls.

We talked about everything, nothing, all things…

Her nickname growing up had been Tissa—a boy teased her about it and she beat him up. Her grandmother made the best teacakes in Louisiana. She first met my father when he hit her in the head with a baseball… accidentally, he said, but she wasn't so sure. She used to rub lemon juice on her face every night, trying to get rid of her freckles. She thought Rhonda Marie would be a good name for the baby if it was a girl. Her sewing club, The Busy Bees, would be meeting at our house in two weeks, and what would we cook, maybe a ham?

And I asked questions: why were Catholics the only ones who would go to heaven? Why wasn't my hair black like yours? Why couldn't I ride my bike around the block? What exactly was a virgin? (That one made her drop her knife in the sink and sit me down for "The Talk.")

She listened. She listened to my dreams of going to college and becoming a teacher; to my complaints about not being allowed to do the same things as my brothers, just because I was a girl; to my adventures with friends from school. There was nothing I ever said I wanted to attempt that she discouraged, no idea expressed ever belittled. She made me feel that what I said was important, that I was important.

I listened. I listened to the rare stories she told about growing up in Opelousas, Louisiana with her brother Elton, and how they kept each other safe during incredibly difficult times. Their mother, my grandmother Eva, died two days after Elton's birth. Poisoned, it was said but never proven, by the wife of their white father, Willie Clopton.

They were raised by their grandmother, Eva Chapman, a good woman who did the best she could. But Elton and Zannett were burdened with the double prejudice of being too white to be black, and too black to be white. Teased and bullied, they learned to fight if they had to and run when too badly outnumbered. Great Grandma died of cancer when my mother was 14 and my uncle 13. The two went to live with their aunt Sylvinie, known as Nanny. Leaving Louisiana, they moved with her to Arizona, Texas, and finally, to the tenements of Chicago.

"It was a hard life," she said, her body tense and still, eyes turned inward in reflection and remembrance. "Sometimes I don't know how we made it."

I held my breath, waiting for more, but it did not come, not about her youth, those times, that pain. We stood like that for a time, her lost in thought, me waiting. A slight shake of her head, a brief smile, I knew the moment had passed.

Mama plucked a knife from the dish drainer and turned her attention to the chickens in the sink. She cut the poultry into 13 pieces: two legs, two thighs, which she always called short thighs, and two wings. The breast was halved and quartered, the back cut in two, and the neck made 13. The liver, hearts, and giblets came in a separate small paper bag. Too young for the use of the knife, I washed each piece and put it carefully into the colander. I salted the parts, she added pepper, and we filled the large red and white polka dotted Pyrex bowl from the pantry with the seasoned meat. The bowl was covered with wax paper and refrigerated.

"Turn the coffee to a click," my mother said. I knew it was time for a break. Normally this meant a cup of coffee, with two teaspoons of sugar and Pet milk added, creating a caramel-colored drink, and of course a cigarette, Lucky Strikes. But this time, she settled for just the coffee, having given up smoking during the pregnancy, something she did for each of us.

I spent an hour or so riding my bike and playing up and down Second Street with the rest of the neighborhood urchins, returning in time to help make Sunday dessert. It was going to be plain cake. My mother learned the recipe from Nanny, who learned from her mother, who in turn learned from her mother, my great-great grandmother. I know the recipe was written down somewhere, but like my mother, I knew the ingredients by heart: two and a fourth cups of flour, one cup of sugar, a half cup of butter, a teaspoon each of salt, baking powder, and vanilla or lemon flavor, three eggs, and a cup of milk. It was a mixture that could be made in layers and iced with butter cream—or jelly when times were lean—or baked in a tube pan, which meant it was going to be the recipient of some kind of fruit and topping.

For this Sunday, the cake was going to be topped with home-canned peaches from the fruit cellar and freshly made whipped cream. We had a well-used Sunbeam mixer that sat on the grey cabinet right inside the kitchen door, but for this cake, my mother most often used a wooden spoon and a large brown earthenware bowl. I was allowed to measure and stir together all the ingredients before Mama took the bowl. Sitting it on her hip like a young baby, she created a circular motion with the spoon, whirling the mixture around in the bowl with speed and precision. The batter smoothed out and turned a pale yellow before she poured it into the greased and floured silver tube pan. The cake baked at 350 degrees for 40 minutes, filling the house with the rich, warm, wonderful smells of butter and sugar.

While the cake cooked, I stood on a stool at the kitchen sink and washed greens fresh from the garden of family friend Roy Burton. The cleaning of greens was a fairly simple process: fill the sink with cold water, plunge the greens in and push them down, take them out, drain the dirty water, fill the sink again and repeat the process. It took about seven water changes to get out the grit and dirt. Time well spent, because there is nothing worse than gritty greens, or better than collards seasoned with ham hocks, salt, and pepper, and slowly simmered till tender.

Sunday dinner was a fabulous feast, but Saturday's meal was always fun. We could count on one of three choices: hamburgers and French fries, tacos, or what we called cowboy food—pork chops and pork 'n beans. Today it was the latter. My mother was a firm believer in pork being thoroughly cooked, and the chops were hard and crunchy. We sat at the table: my brothers, Les, Ronald, and Wayne, and I, crunching meat, shoveling in beans, and mouthing off at each other.

The four of us escaped for the final late afternoon hours of ripping and running with friends in the neighborhood. It was, in truth, escape for all of us. We played, and our mother had a quiet house for a few hours.

Entertainment for my mother was provided courtesy of Michigan Bell Telephone Company. There are numbers that one can always bring to mind: birth dates, social security digits, anniversaries, age. Seven-five-two-one-three-three-two were the magic numbers that made our telephone ring. It rang often, and almost always the call was for my mother. Zannett had a wide range of friends, the result of membership in two social groups, The Busy Bee Sewing Club and The Baker's Dozen Bridge Club. She was also an active parent at St. Joseph's Catholic Church and School, where two of my brothers and I were enrolled.

All of this made for a lot of phone calls, given and received. The black rotary-dial telephone's place was in a small alcove in the dining room, but it rarely rested there. The cord—yes, I did say cord—was long enough to reach the dining room table in the center of the room, and the sewing machine standing in the right front corner.

My mother sat at the dining room table sipping coffee, talking to her best friend, Elizabeth Daniels. Their daily conversations were long and laden with laughter. Sentences often started with, "Girl, let me tell ya," a sure signal that the latest gossip was galloping down the phone lines.

Liz and Zannett's friendship went back to the 1930s, when they had both landed in Saginaw—Zannett following my father, and Elizabeth hot on the trail of her husband Ruben. Those had been wild days for two young beautiful women, and their bond was unbreakable. They did not visit often, but their phone calls to each other were a daily ritual. There had been an occasion when both women called the other several times in a day and were unable to connect. Worried, my mother got in the car to drive to Elizabeth's house to check on her. Elizabeth, also worried, decided to drive to our house. The two saw each other in their cars halfway between houses. They parked, got out, hugged, and laughed. It was a tickler between them for many years.

Meanwhile, I had fun with friends on our street. We all know the International Get In The House Rule: be home when the street

11

lights come on. As dusk settled over the neighborhood, you could hear the sound of children streaking homeward and yelling:

"Bye, see ya tomorrow."

It was time for baths and bed, events that involved much whining and complaining. My father would be home from work and was once again at the kitchen table, this time having his dinner, feigning oblivion to the commotion involved in bathing and bedding four children.

The final dishes washed, the downstairs lights dimmed. Mama climbed the stairs, first checking on each of us, saying goodnight. A soak in a hot bath, fresh gown and duster. Smelling of Ivory and Cuticura soaps, she descended the stairs, turning left into the big first floor bedroom. She hung her duster on the hook in the small closet and sat on the side of the big four poster bed. Sliding her feet out of the white Daniel Green slippers, she swung her feet up off the floor and into bed beside my father. The last steps of Saturday.

Zannett: Part 2

I love fried chicken. Fried, not baked, not broiled, not broasted (whatever that is). Chicken, not nuggets, not strips, not strange unidentifiable pieces. Lightly floured legs, thighs, breasts, and wings fried in a big black cast iron skillet filled to the brim with flaming hot lard! Now that's what I'm talkin' 'bout!

My mother, Zannett Clopton Ramsey, made the best fried chicken in the entire world. Period. No argument, no discussion. She started with three freshly dressed chickens, purchased Saturday morning, from Wier's Poultry Market. She cut each bird into 13 pieces, seasoned them with salt and pepper, and let them marinate overnight in the refrigerator.

Fried chicken was the main attraction in the all-star food lineup that was Sunday dinner: greens, cornbread, macaroni and cheese, fried corn, rice and gravy, and the chicken, of course. For dessert, there would be plain cake and home-canned peaches topped with freshly whipped cream. Much of the preparations had been done on Saturday by my mother and me, so Sunday was about the cooking and eating.

Sunday morning was a quiet time at 720 Johnson Street. My father and my brothers—Les, Ron, and Wayne—slept in. Even our three-legged cocker spaniel, Skipper, snored softly under the dining room credenza. Always an early riser, I knew the cooking agenda and wanted to be part of it. Teeth brushed, face washed, still in pajamas, I went downstairs through the living and dining rooms into the big warm kitchen at the back of the house.

"Good morning, Macki," my mother said softly. "Did you brush your teeth and wash your face?"

Always the same question, always the same answer.

"Yes Ma'am. Good morning, Mama."

At age nine, I already knew a lot about cooking. Knew recipes by heart, knew how to select fresh produce, meat, and fish. I knew because I did these things with my mother on a daily basis. I spent a lot of time with Zannett Ramsey, listening, watching, helping.

I arrived in the kitchen just in time for the gravy making. The necks, backs, giblets, and livers were sizzling in the skillet, leaving a dirty blond residue in the bottom of the pan. My mother had already cut up the seasonings: celery, onion, green pepper, and garlic. She added flour to the pan and handed me a large wooden spoon. I swirled the flour and grease around in the pan, keeping in mind the rules of the rue:

"You burn the rue, you burn the gravy."

The mixture browned quickly, turning a deep rusty reddish-brown. The seasonings *whooshed* as they were added, releasing a wondrous smell that filled the kitchen. Water, always cold, was the final ingredient added at just the right moment, and gravy was born, a rich brown bubbling broth.

Bending over the pan and taking a sniff of the mixture, my mother said, "When I was growing up, a pan of gravy could last a whole week. My grandmother just kept adding water each day. By Thursday, it was really just flavored water being poured over the rice. But that's what we had and that's what we ate."

Statements like that opened for me the window to my mother's past. In hindsight, I realized two things: we always had enormous amounts of food served at our house, the portion sizes two to three times the size of those recommended today, and the children of the house were never made to eat things we didn't like.

"If you don't want it," my mother would say, "that's okay, just don't put it on your plate."

We could and did take a teaspoon-size sampling of food and say, "No, thank you."

As a child, I liked two vegetables, corn and greens, while my older brother Les liked everything—except blackberries, because of the seeds. Ronald, the pickiest of us all, disliked too many things to name. Wayne didn't like bananas, and my sister Kim didn't much care for cantaloupe.

While the gravy simmered, the water in the big stock pot on the back burner began a gentle boil. Two large smoked ham hocks and the greens—washed clean and refrigerated by me on Saturday—were added. The fire turned low, the pot covered.

Mama left the kitchen and went to the large first floor bedroom she shared with my father. She dressed quietly, donning a black skirt, pale-blue short-sleeved collarless maternity top, and low-heeled black leather pumps. For a small woman, Zannett had a surprisingly large head. She bought her hats at Deibles Department Store downtown, where they had a small selection of millinery in large sizes. My mother referred to it as the pumpkin head department. (My daughter, Ashleigh, and nephews, Elton, Jason, and Michael, have inherited the pumpkin headedness from their grandmother.)

She put on her latest purchase, a plain black pillbox with netting in the front, did her makeup—Coty face powder and bright red lipstick. Her black purse and white gloves in hand, she was ready to leave for nine o'clock mass at St. Joseph's Catholic Church.

Instructions were given: Turn the gravy off in 20 minutes, bring two jars of peaches from the fruit cellar, keep your eye on the greens and add water if they get dry, start getting get ready for church.

Our family converted to Catholicism when I was seven. We had been members of Bethel African Methodist Episcopal Church for many years. My father met a Black priest, Father Martin de Porras, when he came into the barber shop for a haircut. They became friends, and we became Catholics, attending Sunday Mass at St. Joseph Catholic Church.

At the time, the only difference I could really see was that the service was shorter, 45 minutes beginning to end, and there was no Sunday School. Although we did sometimes attend Mass as a family, it was often a three-part deal. My mother went to early Mass, my father at 10:30, and my brothers and I went to the noon service. I really think this arrangement came about because we lived in a house with six—soon-to-be seven—people, and one bathroom.

It was the only day in the week when we were all expected to make our own way through breakfast. My brothers and I had cornflakes and milk, my father made eggs and toast. By the time my mother got back from church, Daddy was ready to leave. My mother changed out of her church clothes, replacing them with a blue flowered floor-length duster, and went back to the kitchen.

She lifted the top on the pot of greens, sniffed, added salt, pepper, and a bit more water, and replaced the lid. Twelve ears of corn had been shucked the day before and Mama cut the corn from each cob. She heated bacon drippings in a 14-inch iron skillet and added the corn, salt, pepper, and a healthy pinch each of flour and sugar.

I had no idea why, but we didn't have macaroni and cheese when I was a child; we had spaghetti and cheese, and all the other ingredients were the same. The dish started with a rue of flour and butter. Cold milk was added, then a medium sharp cheese, and salt and pepper. When the cheese melted in the warmed milk, the sauce was poured over cooked spaghetti noodles, cheese slices covered the top and the casserole baked in a 350-degree oven for about half an hour.

My mother in her kitchen was a choreographed dance, beautifully timed. Never hurried or rushed, she moved from stove to sink to refrigerator to table, gathering ingredients, stirring things together, adding seasonings, turning the fire on the stove to just the right temperature to make a gentle simmer, or bubble and boil. She rarely measured anything and when giving me directions, she talked in terms of pinches, dabs, and pours: "Put some flour in the bag, add a pinch of salt, it needs a dab of butter."

And I understood what she meant, because I saw her do it time and again. She didn't taste what she cooked, but was guided by how each dish smelled and looked. I asked her once how she learned to cook.

"The same way you're learning," was her answer.

Today, more than 60 years later, I rarely, if ever, taste what I cook, but rather use my senses of smell and sight. It seems to work.

Back then, at 11:30, Les, Ronald, and I left the house to walk the mile or so to Mass; one block down Johnson, a left turn on

Third Street, six blocks down Third, past the Barber Shop, across the railroad tracks to Sears Street, a right turn on Sears, and three blocks down to church.

We were usually back home by one, and were greeted by the delectable smell of frying chicken. The six-inch-deep, 14-inch-wide cast iron skillet called the chicken fryer was going full blast. The lard was hot and the poultry sizzling. The bun warmer was already half full of crispy golden fried chicken, and by the time the last piece was done, it would be piled so high, the cover wouldn't fit. I assumed everyone made chicken like my mother. That was just not so. She had been taught to keep it simple: salt, pepper, dusted with flour that had just a pinch of paprika added. Knowing when to turn it over, how hot to keep the flame, came with time and practice.

We ate at the dining room table on Sundays and Wednesdays, my father's days off, and while the last of the chicken fried, I set the table with the good china, helped fill serving dishes, and sat them on the table. Daddy sat at the head of the table, nearest the French doors that led to the sunporch. I sat to his left, Les to his right, Ronald next to me, Wayne across from Ronald in his highchair, my mother opposite my father, seated closest to the kitchen.

My father said grace, and we dug in. Dishes were passed, plates filled, knives, forks, and spoons clicked and clacked against the china. Table conversation varied: school, the Sunday sermon, what happened at the barber shop, names for the new baby. Les, Ron, and I had vetoed Rhonda Marie in favor of Kim Zannett for the girl's name and Brian Keith for a boy. As always, the food was fabulous.

The rest of Sunday for my mother was a day of rest. My brothers and I were in charge of cleanup, a duty we put off until late in the evening. Mama very often took a nap or read the paper, talked to friends on the telephone, sewed, wrote letters to family in Chicago, Detroit, or Greensburg.

Two weeks later, our Sunday evening path took a different turn. My mother went into labor. At nine years old, I can truly say that, "I didn't know nothin' 'bout birthin' no baby," and my understanding about how they were made was not even close to the reality.

The impending birth was not the wild, crazy event often portrayed on television sitcoms, where everyone rushes about in hysterical confusion. Mama came out of the bedroom after talking to Daddy, announced that she was going to the hospital, and gave instructions. Les was in charge, we were to go to bed at the usual time, and Aunt Laura was coming to stay until our mother came home with the baby. My father carried the small suitcase that had stood by the bedroom door for several weeks and escorted our mother to the car for the trip to Saginaw General Hospital.

Les, Ron, and I were excited about the baby. We were also a little nervous about the impending arrival of Aunt Laura.

Laura

No one would describe Laura Dudley Bristol as a sweet old lady. She fussed at everyone about everything, and hated our dogs—Skipper, who ignored her, and Guy, who bit her. She professed to be allergic to most things and would stick her fingers up her nose and leave the room whenever a cigarette was lit. My father always called my great-aunt, Auntie. She was his mother's older sister and a major force in our lives. She cared deeply for my father and was very attached to my mother and the five of us.

Aunt Laura had "money," as people would say. During World War II, she had worked in the factories in Detroit as a pattern maker, scrimped and saved and bought stock in GE and RCA in the early years of their operation. She owned, among other things, the two-flat on Epworth Boulevard in Detroit where she and her husband, my uncle O'Brien Bristol, lived on the top floor above her tenants, Ethel and Horace Banks.

My great-aunt set her ways in stone and rarely changed her mind once a decision was made. She believed that Mercury was the best car made and paid cash for the big four-door, shiny black sedans every other year; Borden's was the best brand of drinkable milk; Frigidaire, the only appliances allowed in her kitchen. And she shopped almost exclusively at what was to her THE department store, J.L. Hudson Company on Woodward Avenue in downtown Detroit.

She had a wonderful sense of style and knew what should and should not be worn—what was the latest fashion, fad, or trend. Always meticulous, her suits were tailor-made and beautifully cut. She carried white gloves and wore soft cloche hats when she went out. In the winter, she wore peach-colored woolen underwear, quilted bathrobes, and soft black leather slippers made by Daniel Green.

Her table was elegantly set with fine china, crystal, and polished silverware placed precisely on a spotless linen tablecloth. Fear of dropping, spilling, or breaking made Thanksgiving dinner at her house a nerve-wracking experience for both children and adults. That fear was offset by the deliciousness of the meal and abundance of the leftovers we took home.

O'Brien Bristol—who always referred to his wife as Mrs. Bristol, never Laura—was a man pecked by the hen. A native of Trinidad, he spoke with a clipped British accent, wore black, three-piece pinstriped suits and kangaroo gaiters, and ate everything—including hot dogs—with a knife and fork. He was a journeyman at the Ford Motor Company—no small feat for a Black man in the 1950s. In his youth, he had worked on the Panama Canal, immigrating to the United States in the early 1920s.

Uncle O.B., as we called him, was friends with Marcus Garvey and a founding member with Garvey, as well as others, of the Universal Negro Improvement Association (UNIA), a Black nationalist fraternal organization. I knew little about the organization, except that my uncle met with the group every Sunday afternoon, and that much of his dinner conversation was centered around what Negroes (the politically correct term of the day) needed to do to better themselves and compete in the white world that was America of that time. He preached hard work, persistence, and education, a sermon that continues to be delivered today in the Black community. I didn't think he was really afraid of Aunt Laura, but there was little doubt about who was in charge of their household.

Do not let the picture I am painting here give you the wrong idea. We loved our Aunt Laura very much and the feeling was reciprocated. She smelled like face powder, lilac water, and old people. Her soft brown, wrinkled skin was the color of tea kissed with cream, her bluish-grey hair fashioned in soft curls around her face. She made the best stewed chicken you have ever tasted, had a wicked sense of humor, and told a great story. My brothers and I spent many weekends with her in Detroit, and it was her generosity that helped send my older brother Les and me to college. She also contributed the start-up money for the grocery store my parents opened in the early '60s.

And she could sew! Oh my, could Aunt Laura sew, a magician making magic with needle and thread. Little scraps of colored fabric morphed into shirts, skirts, dresses, and coats with tiny crystal buttons and frilly lace collars for my sister Kim and me.

She would take the bus to J.L. Hudson's on Saturday morning and stand staring at the display windows, eyes narrowed, lips pinched, memorizing every line and detail of the latest fashion draping the mannequin. The fabric and notions purchased on the third-floor fabric department at Hudson's, she returned home to recreate the pattern from memory and make an exact replica of what she had seen. A master seamstress, Aunt Laura said she hated home-sewn clothes that looked "mammie made." She took great pride in her workmanship; every seam was perfect, each dart stitched just so, and the materials were the best that could be found.

Her coming to Saginaw to stay with us during my mother's hospital stay was, to me and my brothers, somewhat mind boggling. Under normal circumstances, we went to her in Detroit for Thanksgiving and Easter, and she came to us in the fall.

Once a year, Aunt Laura came to town and stayed with us for about a week to help my mother with the sewing. Zannett Clopton Ramsey, my mother, was no slouch herself with a needle and thread, and the result of their collaboration was wondrous; the clothing they made for us was amazing. There was, however, a hidden agenda: The Busy Bee Sewing Club and the annual apron-selling contest.

The Busy Bees were a group of women who got together once a month for meeting, eating, and sewing. They had a short meeting, settling the business of the Busy Bees, ate a big dinner prepared by the hosting member, and got down to the business of sewing and gossiping. The membership fluctuated, but the founding group of Cherry Shivers—Johnny Hinton, Mary Eddington, and my mother—remained constant. Their big fundraiser for the year was the making and selling of aprons. At no time was it ever said aloud that there was a contest going on to see who could sell the most aprons, but everyone knew the truth of it. There most definitely was a contest, and Laura and Zannett were determined to win!

My Aunt Laura came to town in the big black Mercury driven by Uncle O.B., armed with remnants of fabric, lace, and other bric-a-brac that she put aside all year for aprons. My mother pulled her apron-making ammunition from the chifforobe drawer in her bedroom and the sewing began. Their weapon of choice was the top-of-the-line Singer sewing machine which sat in a corner of the dining room of our house at 720 Johnson Street. Rarely closed, it was most often overflowing with my mother's project of the moment. It had all kinds of secret drawers and compartments. Some held bright-colored threads, others snaps, buttons, bias tape, pins, needles, and other accoutrements of the craft.

Unlikely patterns and fabrics came together, touched with lace, ribbon, and bright shiny buttons. Some had pockets and tied in the back. Others had a circlet that fit over the head, creating a bib effect. Their aprons were famous and many people had standing orders from year to year. We are talking about the 1950s—the heyday of the apron. They were a part of the female wardrobe and women wore them constantly. Most women had aprons for parties, holidays, and everyday use.

I loved watching and listening to my mother and Aunt Laura. I was sometimes the model for a work-in-progress, standing on a chair, revolving slowly while they nipped and tucked and pinned. They snipped and stitched and talked and laughed, and sometimes cried.

Aunt Laura talked a lot about an incredibly perfect child named Hazel, who never, ever did anything wrong. (It was many years later that I learned Hazel, who died of tuberculosis at age 12, had been her granddaughter, the only child of her only child, Lady.) She spoke too of her sister, my grandmother Alice, and how she was gentle and kind, and died before her time. She told of how the two played as children in the backwoods of Greensburg, Louisiana, how it was growing up dirt poor in the South in the late 1800s, with candlelight, outhouses, and no running water.

There was a saying in the South that you could say just about anything about a person, as long as you started or ended with the phrase, "Bless her (or his) heart." So, you heard a lot of phrases like, "She was ugly as sin," or "I never liked her," and "I'm glad she's dead... Bless her heart."

Every afternoon, Aunt Laura took a nap and the whole house walked on cat's feet, tiptoeing softly, and talking in whispers. Usually, my mama had a quiet cigarette or two and a caffeine kick from a cup of coffee lightened with Pet milk and sweetened with sugar, poured from the small pot that was a fixture on the back burner of the kitchen stove.

After dinner, the sewing continued into early evening, the pile of completed aprons growing, the dining room table a jubilant jumble of colorful scraps. I had no idea how many aprons were made. From my child's eye, it looked like thousands. At week's end, Uncle O.B. returned, and he and Aunt Laura took Highway 10 south to Detroit. Over the next two weeks, the aprons were sold, and at the next meeting of the Busy Bees, the sales were tallied and money counted.

When my mother came home from the meeting, she went straight to the telephone. It was one of the rare occasions from my childhood that I could remember a long-distance phone call being made when there was no birth, death, or other emergency.

"Aunt Laura," my mother said into the phone, "we won again."

Laughter, giggles, and many "bless her hearts" were slung across the telephone wires between Saginaw and Detroit.

I absolutely cannot sew—not a button, hem, or dart. But I know that a seam should be five-eighths of an inch, I can identify most fabrics by touch, and I can spot something poorly sewn a mile away. And I still have the Singer sewing machine, its drawers still filled with threads and snaps and bias tape. It sits in a corner of my family room and is rarely opened, but holds inside the most wonderful memories of both my mother and my great Aunt Laura.

Bless their hearts.

Although my brothers and I were surprised by her visit, I was sure she and my mother had things prearranged, because Aunt Laura arrived bright and early the next morning dressed to the nines and full of fuss. My father had come home in the wee hours to announce the arrival of Kim Zannett, so we were all still abed when the big black Mercury pulled into the driveway with Uncle O.B. at the wheel. Aunt Laura streamed in and the hustle and bustle began.

"We will," she decreed, "get this house in order before your mama and the baby come home."

And we did. For the next four days, there was scrubbing, washing, dusting, picking up, and putting away. Uncle O.B. had returned to Detroit, and my father escaped each morning to the barber shop. That left the four of us and Skipper, the dog. Wayne was too young, Skipper mysteriously disappeared, so Les, Ronald, and I were it. Aunt Laura grumbled and nitpicked and often said:

"You are getting on my nerves."

The feeling was mutual. But there was also praise and "atta-boys," and funny stories about an old man named Jake Knox who would scare her and her sisters when they were children.

And she made stewed chicken and fried corn with sweet green bell peppers. Lester was dispatched to Weir's Poultry to purchase a stewing hen. Aunt Laura cut it into the 13 pieces, washed and patted the pieces dry. She dredged each piece through flour, seasoned with salt, pepper, and paprika. The meat was browned, not cooked through, in about a half-inch of grease poured from the little can on the stove into the cast iron skillet. The browned pieces were removed and set aside. Flour was added to the skillet to make the rue. Cut up celery, green pepper, onion, and garlic were added when the rue arrived at the deep, milk chocolatey-brown color. When my aunt added the cold water, the mixture bubbled up and said, "*Whaaaaa*," sounding as though it were cheering her on. The chicken was returned to the pan, the big skillet was covered, and the fire turned to a click.

The making of this dish sounded and looked a lot like the Sunday dinner gravy. But it was not at all the same, because the mix simmered slowly for several hours, it had a much deeper, richer flavor, the pieces of chicken were larger. But by the time it was done, the meat fell off the bone and melted in your mouth.

I asked Aunt Laura what was the difference between a frying chicken and a stewing hen. With a perfectly straight face, she said:

"A frying chicken is like you, young and quick and tender. A stewing hen is like me, old and tough, but smart enough to have survived a long time." She stuck her hands in her armpits, flapped them up and down, cackled like a chicken, and roared with laughter. I did the same.

We settled down after a bit, finishing dinner with the making of rice and fried corn. The difference between Aunt Laura's fried corn and my mother's was small but mighty. Aunt Laura added finely chopped green pepper to her mixture, creating a very different flavor. Both corn dishes were tasty, but I must confess, I liked my aunt's better.

This was the meal that welcomed home my mother and sister. The revolving door had not yet been installed in hospitals, and women stayed four to seven days after a birth, rather than the 24 hours allotted to today's new mothers. I don't think I was seeing the same thing my mother and aunt saw when they looked at my sister. They cooed and coochie-cooed at her, smiled, and said she was beautiful. To me, not so much. She looked like a Pepto Bismol-colored Winston Churchill. She had more hair than Winston, a smooth soft black cap of it, and big dark eyes that looked at you as though she knew all about you, knew all that you knew.

Our phone rang a lot that day. Friends and family called with congratulations and questions. It was a happy day, made happier by two things. My Aunt Laura, bless her heart, was leaving, and my Uncle Elton was coming, bringing with him two of my favorite women in the world, Cousin Martha and Aunt Marie.

Martha

Born on the wrong side of several blankets in the Louisiana bayou country, I wasn't exactly sure how Martha Smith Gregory was actually related to me. She was my Aunt J.B.'s half sister. Aunt J.B. was my father's half sister. That makes her my father's half sister's half sister. No matter, she was, and always will be, known in my family as Cousin Martha.

Small and delicate, she probably weighed no more than 110 pounds. She had short wispy hair, and her brown skin looked as though it had been stretched over a delicious, bright red apple, giving it the hue referred to as "redbone." She could curl up in a ball and sleep just about anywhere, a habit she said she developed in her childhood, when poverty and circumstance sent her from pillar to post on an often uncertain journey.

My cousin, like so many others, flowed into Chicago in the early 1930s, looking for the chance to change the cycle of poverty and prejudice, and find the elusive good life. She found her husband, Ruben Gregory, known as "Greg," and work as a housekeeper and sometimes a caregiver for wealthy, white Chicago suburbanites. Martha loved to gamble, as well as play bingo, poker, and the slots, and often traveled to Wisconsin where she would wager all day, then reboard the bus and motor back to the city. She lived her life to the fullest, but had a restlessness about her that made you feel she was still seeking that nebulous pearl of peace and contentment.

Cousin Martha wore vibrant colors and high-heeled strappy sandals studded with rhinestones. Her hair color was always a surprise, sometimes brown or black, occasionally bright red or blond. You always knew when she was tickled, because her laughter was most often preceded by a small shriek, as though she was surprised by what amused her. Her quick wit and wonderful sense of humor made her our favorite cousin, and her visits to Saginaw were a joy and delight.

My Uncle Elton, my mother's only brother, drove straight through to Saginaw from Chicago after closing his Eastside barber shop late Friday evening. With him were Aunt Marie and Martha. With our cousin we knew would come three things: fried fish, colored spaghetti, and the game of Tonk.

They blew into town "'fo day in the mornin'" (this translates to before daylight), setting the dog to barking and the new baby to crying, rousting the rest of the family and me from the restless sleep of anticipation. Hugs, kisses, pats, and tears. Again, the coochie-coos for Kim, a.k.a. Winston. The adults went to the kitchen for breakfast and conversation, and the children went back bed.

A few hours after arriving, Cousin Martha went fishing with Roy Burton. She had a special place she liked to go, a small quiet pond a few miles outside of town. Her fishing buddy, Roy, was a friend she and my father had known since their childhood days in Greensburg, Louisiana. Roy had come to Saginaw before my father and had been the one to urge him to make the move here. She wore an old baseball cap, scruffy pants, and open-toed sandals. She said fishing gave her the time to just sit quietly and talk to an old friend. They returned midday, an old tub filled with catfish and perch.

In the backyard, fish scales danced around her head, landing on her cheeks and eyelashes as the catch was cleaned, filleted, then brought into the kitchen to be rinsed. Dipped in seasoned corn-meal, they turned golden brown as they fried in the big iron skillet filled with grease, poured from the little can that always sat on the stove in our kitchen.

Colored spaghetti was Martha's special concoction. Onions, celery, green peppers, and garlic came together in a pan coated with bacon drippings from the little can. They sizzled gently, onions turning translucent, peppers and celery softening. At just the right moment, two six-ounce cans of Contadina tomato paste were added. Each little can was filled twice with water, gently incorporated into the mixture, and the fire turned low.

As a young child sitting at the big grey Formica kitchen table, my feet dangling inches above the floor, I watched her gracefully move about the kitchen. She talked as she worked, telling stories of playing in the deep woods as a child, stealing kisses from her first boyfriend, and running away from home at 14; how her daddy was tall and good lookin'; and how her grandma took in laundry. She spoke of the children she never had, the sister she raised, and the good husband who loved her.

And all the while, the sauce simmered gently, making soft plopping sounds, small red explosions releasing their aromatic secrets into the air of the warm cluttered kitchen. The sauce was a rich, cadmium-red color, made so by the few drops of soy sauce she added just before turning off the fire underneath the pot. Cooked spaghetti was added and the spell was cast. I don't know why it was called colored spaghetti. It just was. Perhaps it was the color of the sauce, or maybe the color of the cook. The name didn't matter; it was the taste that was important.

After dinner, the dining room table was cleared, the children banished to the upstairs, and the cards brought out. Heads poking through the banister railing in the upstairs hallway, my brothers, Les and Ronald, and I laid on our stomachs and watched the action. Tonk was Cousin Martha's favorite. A simplified form of Rummy, Tonk was originally a street card game played for money. There was money bet—pennies, nickels, and dimes—and those at the table played to win.

But it wasn't so much the game that interested me, as the banter among my family of players. Cousin Martha laughed and teased when winning, and blustered, fussed, and sometimes accused those around her of cheating when she was losing. My father's deep loud voice boomed across the room, my uncle told outrageous stories and jokes, and my mother's soft laughter occasionally drifted our way. The card game continued well into the night, and I fell asleep to the sounds of cards being shuffled and lies being told.

Marie

I wandered into the kitchen Sunday morning and found myself enfolded in the arms of my Aunt Marie. She was a hugger and a kisser and a patter. She called me, "Auntie's little movie star," and was without a doubt my favorite and most loved relation.

Marie Collar Armstead was my father's oldest sister. Actually, she was his half sister. Their mother was my grandmother Alice. My father's father was Stewart Ramsey. My Aunt Marie's father was someone else. Marie was raised by Alice's sister, her aunt, my great-aunt Stell. She lived most of the time in New Orleans, but visited her mother and my grandfather Stewart, whom she called Papa, in Greensburg "now and again."

Shortly after my birth in 1946, Aunt Marie—who was also my Godmother—came to live with us, and was an integral part of our family life until she moved to Chicago seven years later. I had the joy of spending many of my childhood summers at her home on the first floor of a two-story, two-family house on Chicago's South

Side. Her house was always spotless, no dust, no mess, no way. But it was also warm and inviting, a place where I always felt happy, comfortable, and welcome.

Her house smelled like New Orleans. If you have never been there, you can't know the smell and I can't help you. I made the discovery on my first trip to the Big Easy many years ago. The moment I stepped off the plane, it was like stepping into her living room, slightly sultry, faintly floral.

Standing five-foot-nine-inches tall and weighing well over 200 pounds, she had been, in her youth, a "big, stand-up-in-the-road woman." With her two gold-crowned front teeth and jet-black hair pressed and curled, she said that that back in the day, she had been young and good lookin' and that all the young men had sought her out. She dated often in her youth, and married twice. It was her sorrow that, with five pregnancies, she was never able to carry a child to term.

Time and the ravages of arthritis bowed my sweet Auntie's legs and gnarled her hands. She bore the constant pain with remarkable stoicism, and an undaunted spirit. Her daily medications were four Bayer Aspirin, two tablespoons of Geritol, and a big glass of water. Her skin, even in old age, was an ebony stone, smooth and black and beautiful, and her smile turned the sun green with envy. She spoke softly, and cried at the drop of a hat.

But her laughter, now that was a work of art. It bubbled up from deep inside her, forcing her mouth open, her head back. Her body quivered and jiggled, and little high-pitched screams escaped, reached out, and tickled you happy all over. And, when you did wrong, she nailed you with soft brown eyes gone cold and the words, "God don't like ugly." The combination always made you feel small in the heart, and sorry for the hurt you caused her.

During the weekdays of my Chicago summers, I spent the day watching old movies on the big black-and-white television in the living room, while Aunt Marie was in the suburbs cleaning the houses of the rich white doctors, lawyers, and businessmen. She was good at what she did, and those that she worked for, paid her well and treated her with respect.

Her passion was baseball and, on the weekends, we went to Wrigley Field to see the Chicago Cubs, or Cubbies as she called them. With fried chicken and yellow layer cake in a brown paper sack, we rode the bus to and from the stadium. She screamed and cheered, clapped and yelled, referring to the Cubs as "my boys," and the other team as "them bastards." It was a bus trip home from Wrigley Field one warm Saturday afternoon that stayed with me.

The bus chugged along Michigan Avenue, collecting passengers, shoppers laden with packages, parents tugging tired and crying toddlers, young couples laughing and giggling. Among those clamoring onto the bus were three young men whose behavior and dress labeled them thugs. Profanity, loud lewd suggestions, and raucous laughter spewed from the three, fouling the air. I drew closer to my aunt, and passengers averted their eyes, hoping their stop and escape would come soon. Conversation withered and died. We, the many, were held captive by the behavior of three. The leader, made obvious by his size, volume, and the deference shown by the other two, stood close by Aunt Marie. Huddled at her side, I could not see her face, but could feel her body stiffen with the hurt of each word, each gesture, each taunt.

Slowly, painfully, Auntie reached toward the shirt of the young thug towering above her on the westbound bus. He looked down with disdain. She looked up with soft brown eyes gone cold.

"Son," she said softly, "you know God don't like ugly."

I could see the struggle in his eyes, and then, their subtle softening, revealing the child within. The tension left his shoulders, the set of his jaw relaxed. And the words, barely audible:

"Yes Ma'am, sorry Ma'am."

His eyes turned toward his friends and I knew they had changed again, back to hard, angry, and wounded. Aunt Marie's had changed, too: back to soft, gentle, and wise. They left the bus at the next stop, us, two stops later. Holding hands, talking softly, we made our way slowly back to the warm happy place of my summers.

Our Johnson Street kitchen was a comfortable, familiar place for Aunt Marie, and she had shooed my mother from the kitchen to rest and nap with Baby Kim while she took over Sunday dinner preparations.

The meal was the standard Sunday fare with one exception: replacing the plain cake would be one of Marie's specialties—sweet potato bread. Sweet potato bread was not a bread. It was like a pie, but not a pie either, though similar in taste. Aunt Marie said it was something her Aunt Stell had always made. I think it was one of those recipes born out of necessity, or the lack of necessities, namely milk. The dish veered from the path of a pie because there was no milk added, and a bit more sugar.

The sweet potatoes had been boiled and cooled before my arrival in the kitchen. I helped peel the yams while listening to Aunt Marie talk about her current boyfriend, Wade. She said she didn't mind the fact that he tried to look younger by covering the grey at his temples with black shoe polish. What she did mind was the habit he had of speaking in rhyming sentences.

"'Skiddle-de-do, how are you? What do ya know, let's go to the show,'" she said in a deep voice, mimicking the man. And the laughter spilled up and out of her, showering me with giggles.

It took a while, but we got the potatoes peeled and put into a big brown crock ware bowl, adding half a brick of room-temperature butter. I used the potato masher, stood on tiptoes to get leverage, and smooshed the mixture together. Every so often, my aunt would lean over the bowl, checking for lumps.

"A little more," she'd say, and then finally, "That looks fine, baby."

She added sugar and let me stir it in with a big wooden spoon. She cracked three eggs, dropped them in, and picked up the bowl, tucking it snugly between her left arm and hip. That same circular stirring motion my mother used when making the plain cake came into play and the spoon blurred as Aunt Marie whipped the contents into a smooth, thick pumpkin-colored confection. Nutmeg and vanilla were the last ingredients added and after a quick stir, she stuck her index finger into the bowl and took a taste, pronouncing it good.

"Now you taste," she said. So, I stuck my finger into the bowl, then brought it to my mouth. It was sweet and spicy, wonderful. A buttered, nine-by-thirteen-inch glass Pyrex dish was filled almost to the top and put into the oven to bake for about an hour. When the sweet potato bread came out of the oven, it was lightly brown on top and set in much the way of a custard or pudding. Cut into two-inch squares, it could be served warm or cold.

By the time the sweet potato bread was cooked, the kitchen was full again. Babies, children, and adults mingled together. Martha and Marie finished dinner, Les, Ronald, and I wandered in and out, gathering dishes and silverware to set the dining room table, my father and uncle leaned in the doorway, talking loud and cracking wise, my mother sat at the table holding Kim. My brother Wayne had crawled under the table with his bag of bottle caps and sat lining them up like soldiers ready for battle. There was no photograph from that day, nothing tangible. But it was there, in my mind, in who and what I am.

My uncle, aunt, and cousin took to the highway shortly after dinner, as the seven of us stood on the porch waving and yelling farewells. Because I was needed at home to help Mama with the new baby, this had been one of the few summers I had not spent in Chicago with Aunt Marie, and I missed that. But we would be going to the Windy City in about a month to visit my great-aunt Sylvinie, known as Nanny. I do not ever recall Nanny coming to Saginaw. She didn't get out much; that was not her way.

Nanny

Two homes: 44th and Dearborn, Chicago, Illinois; and 720 Johnson, Saginaw, Michigan. Separated by dreams failed, promises not kept, potential unfulfilled.

In her youth in Bogalusa, Louisiana, my great-aunt Sylvinie Harper, known as Nanny, had been a big, beautiful kick-ass woman who liked a good time, and took no shit. Her weakness had been Charlie Harper. Tall, dark, and good lookin', he had a wandering eye, and most often empty pockets. Their union, made legal by common law, was a rollercoaster ride of rich and poor, love and joy, jealousy and anger.

My mother and her brother—my uncle Elton—came as young children to live with their aunt in 1929, after their grandmother died. They stayed with Nanny and Charlie for several years and became a part of the Great Northern Migration of Blacks from the South to Chicago, Illinois. For as far back as I can remember, Uncle Charlie lived near, but not with, my great-aunt and their five children: Arabella, known as Bella; Irma Jean; Junior; Verna Lee; and Iola. At the time of our visit, Bella was married and lived in an apartment nearby. Junior and Irma Jean, both married with children, still lived with Nanny, as did Verna and Iola. It was a full house.

Their home at 44th and Dearborn was a blues song, sadly wailing the lyrics of poverty and discontent. Paint-chipped, bluish-grey, two-storied houses lined one side of the street with tiny, tired, dirt-packed yards and sagging front porches. The vacant lot across the street was an obstacle course of debris, broken bottles, and discarded clothes. The view from the back was the railroad tracks, where trains flew swiftly past in a cloud of black smoke, glad to be gone from this place.

There was a smell here, the smell of un: unwashed, unkempt, uncared-for. And there was violence: done with words, done with hands, done with guns and knives. It crept in at night, left its mark, and vanished with the rising sun. For those who lived here, it was home. A community of people who knew each other well, looked out for and helped one another, whenever and however they could.

Nanny lived here, and for one week each summer, my father drove my mother, brothers, sister, and me to Chicago for a visit, and we became a part of a life so different, yet intricately interwoven into what I knew as the fabric of my reality. That summer was no different. We brought everything: sheets and towels, pots and pans, sugar, flower, and coffee, even the coffee pot. When we left, those things stayed.

My older and middle brothers and I joined the urchins of the Chicago slums and played all over the neighborhood. This presented one of the few times I was not limited by the "around the block rule" and the watchful eye of my mother. We raced under the viaduct, laughing at the eerie echo made by our voices, learned the timing of Double Dutch jump roping, and played tag, hopscotch and marbles, saying, "Fan everything, knuckles down!"

Known as "the rich kids from Michigan," we were targets for bullying, but remained relatively unscathed, due to the protection of my two cousins, Verna and Iola. Verna was big and Iola was quick, and if you touched us, they would touch you. For us, it was high adventure, and we enjoyed every minute of it.

Nanny sat most often in a well-worn armchair in the sparsely furnished front room, her wide hips and sagging breasts covered by a shapeless, wrinkled housedress, feet shoved into shoes with backs bent forward from age and wear. From this vantage point, she looked out the front window with sharp dark eyes encased in a big, smooth, round, caramel-brown-colored face. She didn't bother with makeup, and the comb was passed carelessly through her greying-black hair. Watching the comings and goings of the neighborhood, Nanny missed very little of what went on around her. This may have been due in part to the fact that she had the only telephone in the neighborhood. She charged her neighbors a nickel to make a call, and listened to every word spoken. She called my mother by her childhood nickname Tissa, the only one to do so.

Nanny didn't cook three meals a day. Something unusual to us, but common in her household. She "sent to the store" several times a day, sometimes for cereal or milk, often for hotdogs, which were boiled, slathered with sandwich spread, and served on squishy white bread. The store, under the viaduct one street over, was run by a small white man with a thick middle-European accent—the only person not of color we saw during our stay. You could buy just about anything at his store: moon pies, penny candy, big fat dill pickles, snuff, BC Powder, five cents' worth of flour or sugar, and Nanny's favorite drink, Diet Rite Cola.

When my great-aunt did cook, it was a thing of beauty, and remarkable dishes came out of that messy, junky kitchen in the back of the house. She made the best cornbread you ever tasted, golden yellow on the inside, brown and crunchy on the outside. There were a lot of mouths to feed in Nanny's household and many of her meals were low-cost, high-volume, but delicious all the same. One such meal was red beans and rice and baked neckbones. I was not a big fan of the neckbone. Too much work and not enough reward, but hers were slow-cooked and tender, well worth the effort.

Nanny's journey to the kitchen started when she pulled the metal nail file from her dress pocket, and slowly and meticulously cleaned her fingernails. Her next stop was the bathroom, where she washed and scrubbed her hands much as a surgeon might, then to her bedroom, where she donned a clean, well-worn apron.

Three pounds of red kidney beans had been purchased the day before at the neighborhood store and brought home in a brown paper sack. Mama and Nanny had sat at the kitchen table talking and sorting through them, removing bits of debris and other imperfections, then washing them, and letting them soak overnight in a large pot of water.

The next morning, Nanny sent to the store for two large smoked ham hocks and 10 pounds of pork neckbones. She drained the soak water from the beans, covering them again with fresh cold tap water. Added were the ham hocks, green bell pepper, onion, garlic, salt, and pepper. The fire was turned high and the pot brought to a roiling boil, then turned down to a gentle bubble. My Aunt covered the pot so it could "set to work." They would simmer slowly for a good three hours with Nanny occasionally lifting the lid to take a sniff.

Neckbones cost seven cents a pound, and 10 pounds sounded and looked like a lot, but there really wasn't much meat on the bones. The way Sylvinie Harper made them, you wanted to get every tidbit of meat to be found. You didn't eat them using a tool other than your hands, breaking apart the bones, sucking out the meat. It was a greasy, tasty mess.

Her method of cooking them was fairly simple. She laid them out on a large cookie sheet and seasoned them with salt and pepper. A large onion was thinly sliced and haphazardly strewn over the bones. The trick, she said, was to cook them slowly, so the oven was set at about 275 degrees. Sometimes she turned the pan drippings into a whitish-colored gravy, which was served over rice. At other times, they were slathered with a homemade barbecue sauce. Today, they would be plain.

The big kitchen began to warm up with the oven going, and my mother and her aunt escaped to the back porch, where my mother had a cigarette—now that she was no longer pregnant—and my great-aunt lit up the corncob pipe she sometimes smoked. Nanny sat on an old kitchen chair with her legs spread apart and her elbows on her knees. She had the "shades pulled down," which simply meant her dress was pulled down across her knees. My mother sat on the top porch step, her back leaned against the bannister. She held my sister Kim and kept her eye on three-year-old Wayne digging purposefully in the backyard dirt.

The two of them talked quietly, sometimes laughing softly. They did that a lot during the visit. I had the feeling that their conversations were private, and serious, not meant for children. Though

Nanny was only 14 years my mother's senior, she seemed a lot older. They were, in a sense, parent and child, and my mother showed her a deference and respect that at the time I could not quite understand. There was a sadness my mother felt, that I felt from her. I think it was that this place, this life, was what she had come from. She and my father had worked so hard, sought and found a better life, the life that had eluded Nanny. So, the visits were bittersweet. My mother brought what she could, left what she could.

As the day wore on, the smell of food became a siren's song wafting through the house, onto the front porch, drawing us close. A big pot of long-grained rice had been cooked and, as soon as the cornbread was finished, dinner would be ready. We were talking about sho'nuff cornbread here, not Jiffy or Martha White. Another one of those recipes I knew by heart.

Two cups of yellow cornmeal, a half cup of flower, a teaspoon each of salt, baking powder and baking soda, one egg, and milk. Nanny added two things to her mix that my mother did not: a teaspoon or so of sugar and a handful of pork cracklings. Into a big iron skillet was poured about a fourth of a cup of pan drippings from the small grease can that sat on the stove. The skillet heated in the oven for a few moments. It was removed and half the hot grease was stirred into the cornbread mixture before it was transferred to the skillet. When the cornbread came out, Nanny took a plate and sat it on top of the skillet. She then inverted the skillet and the round, brown corncake slipped effortlessly onto the plate.

Dinner was eaten all over the house. Some sat at the dining table, others on chairs and stools in the living room, kitchen, or on the front porch. The food was beyond delicious. The only thing left over was two small sections of cornbread. Mama and Nanny each took a slice, crumbled it into a glass, and filled the glass with buttermilk. This was something my mother did at home, too. My brother Wayne loved this disgusting concoction and whenever she had it, he climbed into her lap and ate it right along with her. Kim did this later, too.

My mother spoke rarely of her childhood, but the bits and pieces I do know tell me that childhood for her and her brother had sometimes been a desperate struggle for survival. She told me once that Nanny had saved them, and that their love for her, and loyalty and devotion to her, were fierce and enduring.

My father returned at the end of the week, and we hugged and kissed, said our goodbyes, and headed north to Saginaw and home. I loved being in Chicago, taking in the sights and smells, ripping and running with my cousins, listening to Nanny. But nothing was better than home.

And I am home... my home, with my family coming together. There will be hugs and kisses, pinches and pats. And food, of course. Fabulous food.

Part Two

The Barbers

I thought I had lost my way home. The road was a blur, shrouded in fog, the map incomprehensible, leading everywhere, ending nowhere. Several things seemed to be creating roadblocks. I had written and published the stories about the women—Zannett, Marie, Martha, Laura, and Sylvinia—10 years prior, under the title, "Stories from the Kitchen at 720 Johnson." The stories were gentle, the women strong and loving, the memories sweet. I kept trying to follow that same path, and the words and phrases just did not ring true. Slowly, I came to the realization that my perspective was skewed. I was standing in the sandals and high heels of the women, and had not stepped into the wingtips and steel-toed, lace-up boots of the men.

I was anchored in life by home and family, and because I so treasured the life I had as a child, I kept wanting to keep this story sitting on the corner of Second and Johnson Street, in the big, old, messy, four-bedroom house of my childhood. Not possible, no, not possible at all. It may have started there, but most certainly could not stay there.

Stepping onto the path, the smell of lilacs strong and sweet, my heart soared. The memories came crisp and clear. And the journey began.

Charles Otis

The house was quiet this early Monday morning in July of 1958, as my father descended the steps from the upstairs bathroom and turned left into the bedroom he shared with my mother. He dressed for the day: crisp white shirt, navy blue- and red-striped tie, dark blue pinstriped suit, shiny black lace-up gaiters. He retrieved his brown envelope-style wallet, along with a small crinkled brown paper bag from the drawer in the nightstand at his side of the bed, and made his way through the living and dining rooms into the big kitchen at the back of the house.

Charles Otis Ramsey, known by all as Otis, did not ever look like he was in a hurry, his movements always slow and deliberate. Taking his place at the kitchen table in the chair just at the entrance of the kitchen, he sat his wallet on the left and the brown paper bag on the right. My mother was already in the kitchen, putting the finishing touches on Daddy's breakfast of fried eggs, bacon, grits, buttered toast, coffee, and a glass of juice. The bacon crisp, the eggs over easy. The coffee had the slight smell of chicory, and the small, three-ounce glass of grapefruit juice had a tinny taste, a reminder that it was canned, not fresh.

She sat the plate in front of him as I arrived in the kitchen. The rest of the house was quiet, my three brothers and sister still abed. Always an early riser, I had been sitting on the top step near the bathroom when both parents passed by on their way to morning ablutions. In the kitchen, I fixed myself a bowl of Kellogg's Cornflakes and milk, and took my place at the table.

My parents spoke quietly about small things, big things, everyday things. From her, the washing machine was acting up, if it rained the laundry would have to be hung in the basement rather than outside, leftovers for dinner. From him, business was slow at the barber shop, a guy owed him money from a haircut given last week.

They were opposites, my parents, in many ways. Zannett was petite, five-three, 115 pounds; Otis, five-eleven, weighing about 180, long arms ending in baseball mitt-sized hands. Her hair jet-black, he, grey-haired since his youth. She was the color of sweet, rich cream with a dollop of French roast coffee; he, a deep, dark, bittersweet chocolate. Her movements quick and constant, his smooth and measured. My mother did not curse or drink; my father delighted in both.

Monday was always laundry day at our house, as well as many others' in the neighborhood, and my mother went down to the basement to crank up the wringer-style washer and start what would be the first of several loads. My father reached inside the brown paper bag and pulled out his dream book and policy slips, settling in to pick the numbers he would play for the day.

Everybody played the numbers, at least everybody I knew. The numbers game dated back to the sixteenth century Italian Lottery. It operated in policy shops, where bettors chose numbers; the game came to the United States in the early 1800s, and was popular in Italian neighborhoods, known as the Italian Lottery, and in Cuban communities as Bolita (little ball). In Black communities, it was just called "the numbers." No matter what you called it, it was illegal. Everyone knew it was illegal, and everyone played anyway.

The game had many attractions. It could be played for as little as one cent; there were no taxes and bookies could extend credit to the bettor. The idea of the game was simple: pick three digits to match those that were randomly drawn the following day. Those numbers were based on horse races. It was a game of chance, the chance to get lucky, although with the odds of 1,000 to one, your chance of winning was slim to none.

You wrote down your number choices in the little book with yellow and white slips sandwiching a piece of carbon paper. You kept the yellow slip and gave the white slip to the runner, or numbers man, who turned it in to the betting parlor, called a numbers bank or policy bank. Everyone knew the numbers man. He was your neighbor, your friend, your relative. Everyone also knew the chain of command for illegal betting in Saginaw. They, too, were your friend, your neighbor, your relative. My father was their barber.

Daddy played every day but Sunday, only because there were no numbers played on Sundays. Picking the numbers for my father was serious business. He studied his numbers book, which had numbers for everything—your name, your dream, your feelings. How many numbers and how much he played depended on his finances, his mood, his hunch.

"I had this dream last night," he said more to himself than to me.

"About what?" I prompted.

"I was back home in Greensburg, and Mama was making fried salt pork and biscuits. She was wearing a purple dress." He smiled at the memory.

"What number does home play for?" I asked.

"Two-three-four," he answered.

"Is there a number for salt pork or biscuits?"

Smiling, he shook his head.

"No, but we could play food," he said.

"What about purple dress?" I asked.

He turned a few pages and wrote down a few more numbers. Daddy was pretty close-mouthed about how much he bet, how often, and how much he won. A big win meant he would suddenly sport a brand-new suit or coat from Mueller Brothers, a high-end men's store downtown, and new appliances or furniture would be delivered. Small wins would sponsor new bikes, family trips to the drive-in, and bills being paid off.

Breakfast eaten, numbers ready for the numbers man, Daddy went out the door to the basement, down five steps to the landing, and then out the back door to where his new 1958 powder blue Oldsmobile 98 stood parked and ready. We got a new car every two years, or almost every two years, depending on how the money flowed.

He backed out onto Second Street, turned right onto Johnson, went one block, turned left onto Third. Five blocks later, he was pulling into the driveway at Third and Potter Streets. Parking behind the barber shop, he went into the building through the back entrance. Daddy exchanged his suit jacket for a short-sleeved white smock, much like that worn by a doctor. He hung the jacket on the coat rack and flicked on the switches, illuminating the inside, and setting the red, white, and blue barber pole on the outside front slowly spinning in an endless, mesmerizing circle. It was eight o'clock and the barber shop would be open for business in half an hour.

The room was quiet, the soft hum of fluorescent lighting warming up, the scrape of Dad's shoes on the worn linoleum floor. As was his habit, Daddy walked to the big front window, lifted his foot onto the built-in bench, and looked out onto Potter, a street soon to be alive with the hustle and bustle of stores, shops, restaurants, and bars. But in the early morning, Potter was a sluggish riser; shop doors slowly opening, apartment residents leaving for work.

From where he stood, my father had a panoramic view of Potter Street, and it always made him smile. Home was 720 Johnson Street; wife, children, dog, family. But this was his world, his place.

The barber shop was actually on the last block of Third Street before the railroad tracks. Potter Street extended from Washington Avenue to Third Street, where it stopped right in front of the barber shop. The right side of Potter was taken up for several blocks by the Potter Street Train Station. Built in the late 1800s, it was a major freight depot, and the sound of trains rumbling in and out of the station were barely noticed, background music for those who lived and worked in the neighborhood.

Down the right side of the street were several businesses: a record store, Weaver's Dairy Bar and Restaurant, a movie theatre, two grocery stores, three bars, another barber shop, a resale shop, a doctor's office, and a car repair garage. Above several of the businesses were apartments, and the occupants began their exodus, headed toward jobs as factory employees, Pullman porters, cooks, waiters, and day workers. Some stopped for breakfast at Weaver's before starting the day, others walking and riding toward eight-, ten-, and twelve-hour days of good, honest work, jobs not easily come by in the current economic recession.

Almost everyone in this tableau was Black. There were two exceptions, the first being Mr. Ginsberg, a lawyer, whose practice was still housed on the second floor above the drug store. He was council to most of the residents and businesses on Potter Street, my father included. He was known as "the Kike." For the longest time, I thought people were saying kite, and that, to me, made no sense at all. When I realized it was kike, that made even less sense. It would be much later in my life that I would come to understand the significance of the term and disrespect that accompanied it.

So, let's put the words out there. Honkey, cracker, nigger, and boy, when addressing an adult Black male. Words of few letters, but great power when spoken with anger, sarcasm, and hate. Meant to belittle, denigrate. As an adult, I would be a part of the generation that would no longer tolerate it. But this was not that time. Not yet.

The only other white person common to this area was Officer Lyman, the policeman who walked the Potter Street beat. Lyman was a big, burly man with close-cropped brown hair, blue eyes, and a ready smile. This had been his beat for many years, and he was well-liked and respected in the neighborhood. He made it a point to stop into every business each day and chat with the owners and patrons. But if there was trouble, he handled it. My father described him as fair and genuine.

Daddy took it all in, waving to some, nodding acknowledgement to others, then checked his watch as the 8:12 train rumbled into the station. The big blue and gold Chesapeake and Ohio engine hissed and sighed, leaving a trail of wispy white clouds as it slowed to a near stop. The 15 or so freight cars seemed more like 100 as they bumped and clanged, disengaging from the engine, one by one. At 8:30, my father would unlock the front door to the shop, but he liked this bit of time in between, this quiet time, when he could think, reflect, and remember. He thought often about home, and the twists and turns that brought him to this place.

His trip to the barber shop was short—eight blocks from 720 Johnson to 231 Second Street—but his journey in life was a different matter entirely. It started for him on November 8th, 1908 in Greensburg, a tiny town in the back woods of Louisiana. His grandfather, my great-grandfather, was born in slave time. His parents, my grandparents Stewart and Alice, were sharecroppers, eventually scraping together the money to purchase the 40 acres they farmed.

This was a time when lynching was common, life was hard, and getting ahead just did not happen. The house he grew up in had no electricity, no running water, no frills, barely the necessities. Charles Otis was the oldest of their four children together: Leon, Curtis, and Carrie being younger. There were two older half sisters—Marie, and Geneva, known as J.B.—from my grandmother's previous relationships.

My father said his father was a mean, harsh man, made so by a mean, harsh life. I did not know him, saw him only twice, and had very vague memories of those times. At age 16, Daddy decided to leave home and strike out on his own. It took him two tries. The first time, he said, his father caught wind of his thinking on leaving.

"He chased me down on his horse, brought me back, and beat me bad, real bad," Daddy said.

That did not deter him, and two weeks later, on a Sunday, he left for church, but never made the services. Instead, he stuffed his one extra pair of pants and shirt under his coat, and he and a friend hopped a train and rode the rails to what they hoped would be a better life, a logging camp they had heard was hiring. Too far for Grandpa to find him.

He said he did some of everything in those early days, anything to earn a bit, and survive. Daddy said his friend went back home, the work too much, the life too hard. But my father pushed on from place to place, earning a little, learning a lot.

It was there that my knowledge of my father's early life became somewhat convoluted. Neither my father nor my mother spoke often of their childhoods because, for both of them, that life had not been easy. Much of what I learned came from stories told when family was together, or questions asked by the curious child that I was. Sometimes I got answers, most often I did not. What I did know was that my father worked on the railroads and in lumber camps in Louisiana, Mississippi, Oklahoma, Arizona, and Texas. His jobs ranged from water boy and kitchen helper in his early teens to chopping down trees and laying railroad ties as he got older. He was strong, hardworking, and knew when to doff his cap and say "yes, sir" to the white bosses, and when to knock you on your ass if you did him wrong.

In Texas, my father met Charlie Hopper, a few years older and a lot wiser in the ways of survival. Charlie was a hustler, a sportin' man: cards, dice, games of chance. He had an eye for the ladies, and the ladies looked right back. The two became fast friends.

"We got up to all kinds'a mischief," Daddy would say with a grin, but never would explain exactly what that mischief was.

Daddy did not visit Greensburg very often, but sent money home to his mother when he could, and made short visits from time to time. His relationship with his father remained strained and stilted. Grandpa resented his oldest son's leaving the farm, and Daddy resented his father's strict ways and mean temperament. He did, however, often visit his Aunt Laura, his mother's sister, and Marie, his half sister, who both lived in New Orleans.

In 1932, N'awlins was jumpin' to the syncopated rhythms of Louis Armstrong, Kid Ory, and Freddy Keppard, as well as to the slow dancin' to *Jelly's Blues,* and songs *Loud* and *Wrong* and *Big Bad Bill* sung by Edna Taylor, Kitty Waters, and Clementine Smith. The men were rich, the women good lookin', and fun was the main agenda. So, when Charlie Hopper suggested a visit to the Big Easy, Charles Otis was a willing accomplice.

And here came the rather strange "six degrees of separation" thing.

The truth of it was that Charlie wanted to sidestep over to Opelousas to see his woman, Sylvinie Chapman. Sylvinie was my mother's aunt, my great-aunt. She already had one child, Bella, with Uncle Charlie, and another was on the way. In addition, my mother Zannett and her brother Elton had recently come to live with Sylvinie, due to the death of their grandmother, my great-grandmother Eva Chapman. Eva had been the only mother the two children had known. Their mother, my grandmother, had died just days after her son Elton's birth. My mother was 14, my uncle Elton, 11 months younger. My father was 23 years old. He said, once, about my mother, that when he first saw her, he didn't pay her no mind.

"She was skinny and mean," he said, "just a kid."

Two years later, that would change.

With a smile and slow nod, my father relinquished the memories of a quarter-century past and unlocked the front door to the barber shop. His week had begun. Mondays and Tuesdays were slow at the shop; Wednesdays were a half-day. Things picked up Thursdays and Fridays, with Saturdays being the busiest day of the week.

The shop itself was housed in a twelve-by-eighteen-foot space. Through the big picture window in the front could be seen three barber stations, each consisting of a brown leather-padded chair in front of a narrow grey cabinet. The cabinet was a wonderful thing with all kinds of drawers, nooks, and crannies holding the tools of the trade. There were three sets of electric clippers with their long black tails hanging down the front, some plugged in, others waiting to be brought to life. Scissors of all shapes and sizes lined up, hoping to be chosen to snip and shape.

On top of the cabinet was a large white mug holding a cake of soap and a soft short-handled brush; with a few drops of water, and a swish of the brush, shaving cream foamed and bubbled. A tall cylindrical glass jar was filled with a mysterious blue liquid that sanitized combs. And there was the ever-present bottle of Jeris aftershave lotion and can of talcum powder waiting to give the final touch to a shave and cut.

Along the wall across from the barber stations were customers' chairs, a mix of wood, Formica, and plastic. A free-standing ashtray with a distinct art deco look moved up and down the row, collecting the ashes of cigarettes, cigars, and pipes. Heating, when needed, was provided by a large space heater at the end of the row.

My father had the first station, closest to the front window. When Mr. Cantu, the original owner of the shop, had died some years earlier, my dad had taken over ownership and moved from the middle to the front. The name, however, had not been changed. My father said he didn't see the need. The middle chair remained largely unoccupied, with occasional short-timers renting for a while, then moving on.

The third station had been occupied, for as long as I could remember, by Alex Lyda, known to all as Ecky. Ecky was a small, bald man with cream-colored skin and a sad countenance. Quiet and soft spoken, Ecky walked everywhere he went. He and his wife, Mama Rose, lived on the corner of Third and Johnson Street, in a big white house where they took in boarders. We lived one block away, on the corner of Second and Johnson. Daddy had to pass Ecky's house each day on the way to work, but would drive right by him, stopping only if the weather was really bad.

Ecky preferred to walk. The only time any of this changed was when Ecky drank. Liquored up, Ecky was loud, boisterous, and funny as hell. A ride home was an absolute necessity. I didn't know much about my father's relationship with Ecky, and although the two men saw each other every workday, our families did not socialize much. There were times when my younger brother Ronald and I would see

Mama Rose on her front porch and get invited in for ice cream or cookies, but I don't ever recall the Lydas coming to our house.

On a slow summer Monday, the customers were few, and those that came in, lingered to talk. Barber shops were places for posturing, postulating, and pretending, the pretending being very close to outright lying. It was a place where they could relax without the eyes and ears of white bosses or jealous wives and girlfriends turned their way.

I spent a lot of time in the barber shop as a child, so did my brothers Lester and Ronald, and when there, we listened. The rules of children being in the barber shop were the same as those when shopping with my mother. You did not interrupt, did not join in adult conversation, and you never, ever corrected. The conversations were about politics, sports, and man gossip. Sometimes the gossip was juicy: who was not faithful and who got caught at it; who was getting a divorce; who was gambling and how much.

Baseball was huge in our community, played on both a national and local level. My father had been on a team called The Spoilers until injuries forced him to stop. National games were broadcast on the radio. Local league games were hugely popular and teams played a full schedule at Veterans Memorial Park, so there was always some argument over who committed the error that lost the game, or boast about who knocked the ball out of the park, or made a daredevil play stealing home or hitting the grand slam. The place was alive with raucous laughter, shouting, and talking over one another.

But there were serious conversations, too. News coming from the South was both exciting and frightening. The power and influence of Dr. Martin Luther King, Jr. was growing daily: the successful bus boycott in Selma, the landmark *Brown vs. Board of Education of Topeka* decision, and the formation of the Southern Christian Leadership Conference. There had also been the murder of Emmett Till, the bombing of Black churches in the South, and continued and escalating violence by the Ku Klux Klan.

You could feel the anger emanating from these men as they talked and argued about segregation, integration, and their rights having been wronged, generation after generation. All these men had been born in the South, and had been part of the Great Northern Migration in search of something more, something better than their parents and grandparents had. Some talked of having left in the dark of night, running from the law, the law that said they could not eat here, sit there, live or work in a place, enter from the front, earn a living wage. Others, like my father, left family and farms where the work was constant and the life too harsh. And I listened, slowly shedding the innocence of ignorance.

My father had a set of rules that he put into play at the barber shop. I remember them well, having heard them often enough:

- The customer is not always right. My father often said: "A lot of these guys don't know much of nothin'. Don't know what they are talkin' about, don't know how they want their hair cut, ain't got no sense at all about things that are just common sense."

- Don't trust the Big Timers. Daddy said: "If you got to talk a lot about what you got, who you know, and where you been, you probably ain't got it, don't know 'em, and ain't been there."

- If you want it, work for it. "Keep at it till 'ya get it," my father said.

- Do the best you can. "That's all you can do," he said, "all anybody can do."

I liked to watch my father work. He kept up a bit of conversation with the customer in his chair and had a habit of cutting your hair the way he thought it should look, often ignoring your directions or requests. With a flourish, he would shake out the protective blue-striped cloth, covering you from neck to knees. Taking a small, three-by-five-inch strip of white tissue from the box sitting on his cabinet, he would wrap it snugly around your neck before securing it and the coverup with a small metal clip. Pumping the foot pedal at the bottom of the chair, he would adjust your height to get the best view of your head from all angles.

The clippers would buzz like a swarm of angry bees, sliding across your head, and hair would fall away, some to the floor, some onto the cloth. His big hands tipped your head down, up, left, right, according to the need. Each set of clippers had sets of blade heads needed for length and type of hair. And he stopped from time to time, switching from long to short, thick to thin.

Both men and boys wore their hair fairly close-cut in these times and haircuts were a regular weekly occurrence for most. When Daddy had your cut finished to his satisfaction, he would sprinkle powder onto his talc brush, whip off the cloth, and slide the brush back and forth across the newly cut scalp and neck.

It was always interesting to watch what happened when a nearly-bald man would settle into the chair and say, "Don't take too much off the top."

My dad would make sure he turned the customer away from the mirror, took out his scissors and clipped away at the air just above the man's head for a good 10 minutes. Everyone in the shop saw it, but no one said a word.

Hair washing was a very telling event, and I noticed that for some customers, a single lathering with the same Castille soap my mother used at home did the job. For others, Daddy lathered up three or four times. I knew better than to ask at the shop, so I questioned him about it at home and he explained that when the lather was white, the hair was clean, so he kept washing till the suds turned white.

"Some of these guys," he explained, "have dirty jobs in the plant, or on the railroad, and some of 'em just ain't so clean."

So when I was at the shop, Daddy would give me a wink and hold up his fingers before starting the process to indicate how many times it would take to see white suds. To this day when I shampoo my hair, I study the bubbles, checking for clean.

My father cut the hair of all three of my brothers, my mother, and our dog, Skipper. None of them liked it. My brother Les, who was 15 and wanted the current style called a Quo Vadis, never got that, and would wear a hat after a stint in Daddy's chair. My younger brothers—Ronald, nine, and Wayne, five—didn't care. My mother just accepted the inevitable, and the dog hid. Fortunately, I missed the whole thing, because I wasn't allowed to get my hair cut. Black girls under the age of 15 did not get their hair cut.

He was better at the shave. A drop or two of water into the small white cup that held shaving soap, *swish-swish-swish* with a small brush, and the soap bubbled and foamed. The edge of the straight razor gleamed as he slowly scraped it back and forth across the leather razor strap attached to the chair. He would lather up the face and you could hear a very slight scraping sound as razor met skin and slid slowly around the face, a skater on an icy pond. He would squirt a bit of Jeris aftershave balm into his hands, rub them together, and gently tap your face, soothing the freshly cut surface. The soft brush holding the talc swished back and forth around your neck before the cloth was removed and you exited the chair.

When I was a small child, I thought our front porch was enchanted. It most often smelled of lilacs from the trees that surrounded the porch, and things just seemed to magically appear. On Mondays, Wednesdays, and Fridays, glass quart bottles of icy cold Sealtest brand milk appeared in the two-by-three-foot insulated silver box, which sat in the corner just to the right of the top step.

Letters and small packages materialized daily in the black rectangle attached to the siding to the left of the front door. Even Dr. Archer A. Claytor, the family physician, stepped—unbidden, I thought— onto the porch whenever one of the Ramsey children fell ill. But that was when I was a small child.

Now, I knew that the milkman brought the milk, the mailman brought the mail, and Dr. Claytor came if called and the patient was deemed unable to make it to his office. So, it wasn't enchanted, but the front porch was among my favorite places growing up, coming second only to the kitchen of the big four-bedroom house at 720 Johnson Street that I called home.

My father was extremely proud of our house. When many Black veterans returned from the war in early 1945, they chose the inexpensive living quarters offered by the government housing projects. My father had been sending money home during his tour, and my mother banked it all. They bought the house on Johnson Street in 1946, early integrators into the area, and moved in on October 23rd, 1946, three days before I was born.

A twelve-by-twelve-foot concrete rectangle enclosed with red brick, buttressed with tall columns supporting the tiled roof, the porch was a portal through which my family and I entered the safety of home, and ventured out into the world of 1958 Saginaw, Michigan. When my parents moved here, it was pink stucco. When I was about five, the stucco came down and white aluminum siding went up. The porch was painted red, and I don't ever recall a tou-chup or repaint... it just stayed the same.

Because we lived on a corner, we had three distinct views from the porch. Straight across the street was Zion Baptist Church. To the right and across the street was the big white house with red shutters, home of the Greer Family. To the left, across the side yard, were our next-door neighbors, Mr. and Mrs. Gates. On the other side lived the Motens, three sisters and their husbands and children, and a brother. Their house was divided into apartments, two down-stairs, one up.

Porch sitting was a happy pastime of mine, something I could do for hours, watching the comings and goings of every day. The big powder blue Buick Dynaflow, which cruised by every weekday at 4:15, was Mrs. Watson going home from the factory at day's end. I also watched the young biracial teen walking past on her way to Robinson's Laundry to meet her mother, and then their return trip, the two holding hands, laughing and speaking German. There were the apartments across the street, next door to Zion Baptist Church. Always something to see there... Children running in and out, peo-ple coming and going, laughter, bickering, scraps of conversation.

Although my three brothers, Les, Ron, Wayne, and my two-year-old sister Kim sat on the porch, my parents rarely did. My mother seemed to be in motion from early morning to late evening, and sitting down was not a part of her agenda. My father left each workday, returning home in the early evening. He was about the business of providing. Their roles seemed clearly defined. Mama took care of home and children; Daddy earned the money that provided necessities, food, shelter, clothing, as well as extravagances— piano and dance lessons, movies, and weekly allowances.

Sitting on the porch most summer evenings, I waited for my father to come home. The barber shop closed at 5:30 on Mondays, Tuesdays, and Thursdays, and Daddy would be home within the half hour. I saw the car make the turn from Third Street onto Johnson and cruise one block to the corner of Second and Johnson, turning right onto Second and pulling into the driveway at the side of the house. Daddy was home, walking a bit gingerly on feet that ached after the long hours standing at the chair, clipping, shaping, and tweaking the hair of patrons, young and old.

My father was actually of average size, but I thought he was huge... I still think so. He stood tall and erect, as though a drill sergeant had just yelled, "ATTENTION!" He kept his shoulders back, head slightly forward like a turtle emerging from its shell. He had greyed prematurely, something that ran in his family, so I never saw his hair any color other than the salt and pepper mixture, cut in a close crop, buzzed style. Skin, a rich chocolatey brown, smooth and soft to the touch, his face was home to expressive eyes, almost black, sparkling with life.

My father had big baseball mitt hands and his feet looked larger than they actually were, because his shoes were purchased a size larger, he said, to help "ease the ache." He carried the nickname Bones, because he had broken both legs, an ankle, and a wrist playing softball in his younger days. He had said once that he had brittle bones. The brittle got lost and it just became Bones.

Slowly, carefully, he climbed the five steps to the front porch.

"Hey, Mike," he greeted me.

"Hey, Daddy," I answered back and followed him into the house.

We passed through the living room, into the dining room, where he stopped to greet my mother seated at the sewing machine, putting the finishing touches on a sundress for my two-year-old sister, Kim, who crawled around on the floor, happily mumbling to friends seen only by her.

He continued to the kitchen at the back of the house, stopping briefly in the dining room to turn the television to channel five. In the kitchen, he sat in his usual spot at the grey Formica kitchen table. I had already received instructions from my mother about dinner for Daddy, so although I thought of it as fixing dinner for my father, I was actually just heating it up. Monday's meal was always leftovers from the scrumptious Sunday fried chicken feast.

I moved comfortably around the kitchen, getting the containers of collard greens, rice and gravy, chicken, and fried corn from the refrigerator, scooping it all into the pan and turning the stove to a click, which was the lowest setting on the stove. We made small talk, very small. Daddy was not a big talker in our everyday life.

"Were you busy today?" I asked.

"Yep," was the answer.

"I beat everyone at marbles this afternoon," I reported.

"Mmmm," he replied. "Where's the paper?"

I found the paper, dished up his dinner, and left him in peace. My dad ate slowly and deliberately, reading the paper, starting with the sports section, then national, state, and local news, and finally the comics. Looking at that now from the perspective of an adult and former teacher, the everyday occurrence of his reading the paper, or anything at all for that matter, is a marvel.

My father's education stopped at about third grade. I taught third grade for many years and knew exactly what a third grader's reading was like. Clearly my father managed to learn far beyond his formal schooling experience. His lips moved as he read, though he made no sound and, on rare occasions, he would ask me to pronounce a word for him. I never saw my dad read anything fictional. He read the newspaper from front to back every day. He liked the encyclopedias, the Almanac, and a very thick book of home remedies for common health issues. He did not read for pleasure, but rather read to learn.

My mother and I passed each other in the dining room, she on her way into the kitchen to talk with my father, me on my way outside to ride my bike and catch up with friends. There was no such thing as staying inside watching TV on a warm summer evening, and even if there had been, the television was tuned to channel five in preparation for the evening news. The evening news with John Cameron Swazey came on at 6:30, but Daddy tuned to the channel at 6:00. That made no sense, but be that as it may, you did not change the channel. We had, as children suffered through the news program waiting for John Cameron Swayze to say, "Hopscotch in the news," the clue that the program was almost over.

My father's taste in television was well-known. He liked the news, a program called *Victory at Sea*, the *Friday Night Fights* brought to you by Gillette Razor Blades, *The Ed Sullivan Show*, and oddly a program called *Kuklah, Fran and Ollie*, the stars of which were hand puppets.

Although I did not like watching the *Friday Night Fights*, I did like watching my father watch the fights. He would sit on the edge of the big easy chair and lean forward, fists clenched, punching and grunting along with the contenders in the ring, yelling at the referees for not calling what he clearly thought were low blows and late hits.

The shop closed at 1 p.m. on Wednesdays, and Charles Otis was home by 1:30. During the school year, four of us were at school, so the house was fairly quiet, and my father took a nap before we came home to an early dinner. In the summer, this was reversed, and we had an early dinner, then disappeared out into the neighborhood while Daddy snoozed.

We did not sit down to eat together as a full family every day. That happened on Wednesdays and Sundays, dictated by my father's schedule; the barber shop was closed on Sundays and open a half-day on Wednesdays.

The dining room table was set with a tablecloth and everyday dishes. We all took our places, my father at the head of the table, my mother at the other end. Me to Daddy's left, Ronald next to me. Lester to Daddy's right, Wayne next to him, and my sister Kim in the highchair closest to my mother. Although I did not recognize it at the time, meals at our house were prepared in traditional Louisiana style. Onion, celery, green bell pepper, and garlic were usually involved. It also meant there would be rice and hot sauce.

My father loved rice, so it was served about 350 days a year, over peas, beans, greens, and stews, covered in gravies, and sprinkled liberally with Frank's Hot Sauce, known in our house as Louisiana Red. The midweek meal was usually a roast, beef, or pork, with rice and gravy, of course, and a vegetable, maybe two.

At the barber shop, my father was garrulous and animated, talking constantly, holding court, telling stories and jokes, almost as though he was on stage... perhaps he was. At home, he was very different. It was as though the performance ended, and as the curtain closed, so did he. Dinner at our house was a noisy affair with five children chattering and vying for attention, our three-legged dog Skipper slipping around chairs, catching scraps. But my father was, for the most part, a listener, taking it all in, but adding little to the conversations swirling around him.

Being around Daddy on a Wednesday was a lot like playing hide-and-seek or duck-duck-goose. He most often addressed you in commands:

"Bring me this."

"You, there, get me that, go to the store, run next door."

If you happened to be passing by when he needed or wanted something, you were "it," the chosen getter or runner. The worst of these commands had to do with a large, oval-shaped pan, white-rimmed with black. The foot soaking pan.

It was a Wednesday ritual. After dinner, Charles Otis would pluck the pan from the hook where it hung, right outside the kitchen door on the wall of the stairwell leading to the basement. He would fill the pan with warm water and add a mixture of Epsom salts and Ivory Snowflakes detergent, and carefully walk it to the living room. Newspaper was spread out in front of his favorite chair, and he would remove shoes and socks, roll up his pantlegs, and immerse his aching dogs in the water.

My dad had ugly feet and, sad to say, four of his five children—me included—have those same uglies at the ends of our ankles. Long, prehensile monkey toes that curl claw-like, enabling us to pick up large objects with our feet, second toe longer than the big toe, corns, calluses, bunions. *Ewww!*

My father sat comfortably, soaking and listening to the baseball game on the radio for about half an hour. Then came the fun part.

"Get me a towel," he would command to the first passerby.

Out would come the pocketknife and he would begin the process of removing dead skin, slicing and dicing corns, and picking at the hard calluses on the bottoms of his hooves. Once this task was done, my father got up and walked away from the mess all of this made. He would lie in wait, it felt like, for the first of his three older children to come through.

"You, get that water," he would order. Translated, that meant empty the pan, put it back on the hook, gather up the newspaper that held the foot cooties, put it in the waste basket, and drop the towel in the hamper. Again, I say, *Ewww*. My brother Les was adept at disappearing on these occasions, so it was usually Ronald or me who did the disgusting deed.

The words from the blues song *Stormy Monday* made famous by Bobby Blue Bland—about the eagle flying on Friday, and the singer going out to play on Saturday—created a powerful image in the mind of a child. For me, it conjured up pictures of the big American Bald Eagle gliding across the sky, and my friends and me outside running, laughing, playing. The truth was much more adult. Friday was payday, the eagle a reference to the image stamped on the silver dollar, and going out to play was... Well, we're not talking tag or jump rope.

The barber shop radiated a different energy on the weekends, and so did my father. He knew the shop would be busy from early morning till late evening, and there was money to be made. Some would be coming straight from third shifts at one of the three enormous factories—Steering Gear, Grey Iron, and Malleable Iron—places that kept food on our tables and pollution in our lungs. Others arrived midday from businesses large and small—clerks, cleaners, clever entrepreneurs. High lifers, low lifers, they would pass through the barber shop for a shave, a haircut, a trim of beard and mustache.

As a rule, Daddy did not extend credit, but would, on occasion, make an exception. He referred to it as pay-backs, with the strict understanding that the next time you got paid, he got paid. So, a few came in to quietly slip him what was owed.

Work week over for most, the men lingered, in no hurry to get home to wives, children, girlfriends, and responsibilities. There was laughter loud and raucous, jokes told and tall tales shared.

My father was most often at the center of things. He was a wonderful storyteller; many of the tales he told were from his adventures as a young man working in lumber camps across the South. My favorites were the stories about Old Blue. I had heard the stories so many times that I just about knew them by heart. So, for me, it wasn't so much the story, but the teller of the tale. It was like Daddy stepped on stage, an actor drawing his audience in, carrying them off to a place and time far different from the here and now. He took on the voices and gestures of the characters, sometimes loud, sometimes soft. He made you believe, or maybe not believe, but enjoy the disbelieving.

"Old Blue," Daddy would start off, "got his name cuz of his color."

Someone would always say, "You mean to tell me he was blue?"

And Daddy would continue: "Well, no, not exactly. He was big, I mean big, 'bout six-foot-eight, had long arms, hung down almost to his knees, hands big as smoked hams, and feet like them snowshoes Eskimos wear. An' he was the blackest man you ever saw, made him look like his skin was a shiny dark blue. So, we all started callin' him Blue. I disremember what his real name was, think it mighta been Earl. I was 16 when I first met 'em at a loggin' camp in Mississippi, not too far from Jackson. But I'd heard of 'em… everbody knew him. He was famous on accounta cuz he could call trains."

At this point the listeners would object. "Gowan Otis, can't nobody call no train! Man, that's crazy!"

Stepping away from the customer sitting in his chair, Daddy would throw back his head, stretch his mouth as wide as he could, and let loose with a big, booming, "WHAAAAAAAAAAAAAAA!"

Taking a breath, he would do it again: "WHAAAAWHAAAA!"

The shop would grow quiet, everyone's attention on Otis. Just where he wanted it. And the story would continue:

"Well sir, Old Blue had one job and one job only. He called the trains."

Then my father would exclaim:

"*WHAAAAAAAWHAAAAWHAAAA!* He'd call, and them cars would come chugging into the camp to pick up the logs."

Daddy would pause for effect, and lean forward.

"If he didn't call," Daddy said, "the train didn't come. No call, no train."

I waited for the question I knew would come, when someone asked, "Didn't that train have no conductor?"

My father answered: "Don't know, didn't matter. If he didn't call, the train didn't come. No call, no train, plain and simple."

Then my father said, "Old Blue was something special. Everybody knew that, too. He was a kinda sharp dresser, clothes always clean, white shirt, buttoned up to hiz neck, black and red checkered suspenders with shiny gold snaps holding up hiz pants. Had brown boots laced up to the knee. Don't know how he did it, but they was always shiny, looked fresh polished. He slept on the softest bunk in camp, always got served first in the mess tent. And could he eat. Man, you never seen nobody eat like Blue. Twenty pancakes, two pound 'a bacon, a dozen eggs, sometimes two for breakfast. Seen 'em eat three whole chickens without battin' an eye. He got along with everybody, told a good joke, took his share 'a teasin'. So, things was goin' along good till Blue got into it with The Man."

Ears pricked up, heads turned, and the shop got even quieter, the only sound, the subtle hum of Ecky's clippers and the *snip, snip, snip* of the scissors gliding just above the head of the customer in my dad's chair. This was about to get good.

"I guess Blue was acting just a little too uppity," Daddy continued, "and The Man wasn't likin' the attitude of someone who didn't know his place.

"So, one day he says to Blue, 'You gonna hafta do more 'round here to earn your keep, some cleanin', moppin', and haulin' trash.' Said it loud, so everyone could hear."

Then Daddy said, "Blue looked the man up and down, leaned in hands on hips and says, 'Oh, hell no! I call trains, that what I do, that all I do.'"

"You do what I tell ya ta do!" yelled The Man.

"'I call trains, that what I do, that all I do!' yelled Blue right back.

"Well, things went flying downhill after that, and next we knew, Blue balled his hands into big hammy fists, reared back and knocked that peckawood right on his ass."

If there had been an orchestra somewhere on the premises of the barber shop, there would, at this point, have been a "*Da-da-da-daaaa!*" played at staccato pitch. Some of the men in the shop shook their heads; a few "oh, shits" were mumbled.

My father went on: "Well, soon as Old Blue let loose that punch, he knew he was in some mighty deep trouble. The Man was out cold, dead for all Blue knew. They hang you for that, no trial, no judge, just a tree and a rope. So, he took his hat, ran right out the door, disappeared into the deep woods surroundin' the camp."

A sigh of relief rose from the men in the barber shop.

"They looked for Blue for a day and a night, but they dint find 'em," Daddy said. "We knew where he was, tucked up in a rough cabin about five miles into the deep woods. They knew we knew, and we knew they knew we knew. But no one was sayin'."

My father kept his patrons' rapt attention.

"Meantime, work at camp went on," he said. "Trees was cut, logs piled up. Business as usull. 'Cept them trains didn't come. No call, no train, plain an' simple. Them bosses, now they was gettin' riled. They had us all line up and try the call, thinkin' we was all colored, so any of us would do." We tried:

"WHAA, WHOOOOOO, WEEEEEEEAHHHHHH, HOOOOOOOOOOOOTHOOT!"

Then he said, "Nope, not a train to be seen." There was laughter now, and a few even tried the call. They knew Otis was lying, but were caught up in the tale anyway.

"Well, sir, after a week 'a no trains, with logs backed up and stacked up, nothin' goin' out, no money comin' in, the Boss Men knew they was beat. They let it be known that Blue was in no trouble in no way and there'd be a money bonus comin' to each and every man soon as Blue was back on the job."

My father continued:

"Come evenin', we heard it, low and distant at first, then louder and louder. We could see steam slowly rising from the engine of the locomotive. And then the call: 'WHAAAAAAAAAAAAA, WHAAAAWHAAA!' And here come Old Blue, walkin' down the center of the tracks, shoulders back, boots shinin', grinnin' from ear ta ear. The train right behind 'em. When Blue stopped, the train stopped. Then he'd start walking and callin' 'WHAAAAAAAAAAAAA WHAAAWHAAA!' and the train would start chugging. It was a sight to see. Yessir, a sight to see."

For a moment, there was a comfortable silence among the men in the shop. The smiles and distant looks said that they saw it all: Old Blue, the camp, the train, the knockout punch, the triumphant return. My father was that good. Yessir, a sight to see.

The highpoint of the week at the barber shop on Potter Street was Saturday; the comings and goings could make the head spin. A lot of children accompanied parents for the weekly or biweekly cut. The kids sat quietly, while mothers and fathers chatted and gossiped, laughed and joked. Hustlers bolted in and out with scarves, hats, dresses, cigarettes, and other items that just happened to fall off the back of a mysterious truck. Translation: stolen goods.

The barber supply man, Mr. Thomas, delivered bottles of talcum, tissues, fresh towels, coverups, combs, and other miscellaneous items, took orders for the next week, and moved on to other stops along his route.

The numbers man blew in, collecting betting slips, chatting up the customers. My brothers and I were part of the traffic, stopping in to collect four dollars to go to Weir's Poultry at the end of Potter Street to get fresh chickens for Sunday.

And always someone delivering dinners—fish, chicken, tacos, barbecue—sponsored by the church ladies, a sewing club, a group of some sort, or an enterprising individual. With the chicken, fish, or barbecue, you got potato salad, greens or green beans, cornbread, and a hunk of sheet cake. In the taco dinner, there were four tacos, sometimes beans and rice, and a hunk of sheet cake. The sellers stopped in earlier in the week to take orders, and the dinners delivered by car usually arrived around lunch time, served on a Styrofoam plate covered with foil, along with a white plastic fork and knife wrapped in a white napkin.

And they were tasty, the cakes homemade, the chicken and fish crisp and warm, the barbecue slathered in a sweet smoky sauce, the tacos well-seasoned and held together with three toothpicks.

My father never brought food from home to work. I think to him, a lunch pail put him in the laborer category. He saw himself as a business owner, and he dressed and acted accordingly. During the week, Daddy ate at Weaver's Dairy Bar across the street, or Mama Lilly's next door. On the weekends, it was one of the dinners.

Somewhere along the way, a bottle of liquor would appear, sometimes from the inside coat pocket of a customer, sometimes from the bottom drawer of Daddy's cabinet, where paper cups were stored. Drinks were shared, sometimes a few, sometimes a lot. Daddy would have been on his feet for 12 hours or more, a long day. The shop closed at 7:30. If he arrived home at 8:00, a few drinks had been shared. Nine or later meant a lot of drinks. That time difference also determined how his Sunday was going to go.

Sunday was my father's day off, a day of rest. And rest he did. The household tiptoed around until he awoke around 9:00 a.m.

Daddy did not always go to church. Some Sundays made for two pajama days for him. No suit, no tie, no hard-soled shoes. He kept on his pajamas and slippers, and added his robe. Made of heavy lined satin, black with wide silver stripes, and a black belt with tussles on the ends, it was reminiscent of something William Powell might have worn in the 1934 film, *The Thin Man*. He didn't leave the house, slept late, read the paper, took a nap, listened to the ball game.

No matter what my father wore, we ate Sunday dinner as a family. We came together at the big dining room table dressed in a crisp white tablecloth and set with the good dishes garnered from the glass-fronted china cabinet. As I've said, my mother was the best cook in the entire world. Period. So, everything she made was the best you ever ate. And again, most often, Sunday dinner was fried chicken, rice and gravy, spaghetti and cheese, and fried corn, greens or green beans.

But sometimes if she had a project in the works, we had ham. Ham was always referred to as a smoked picnic ham, and for many years, I thought it was called that because it was for a picnic. No matter the reason, it sat on a platter near my father's place at the head of the table, shiny and warm, waiting to be carved. The picnic was almost always accompanied by potato salad and green beans. On the dining room credenza sat a plate of warm fried apple pies, sprinkled with cinnamon and sugar.

The blessing was given, the ham carved, dishes passed, plates filled. The food was good, the helpings large, a thing we took for granted. But the draw of playing outside with neighborhood friends on a sunny summer day was the call of the wild, and we shoveled it in as fast as we could without being disrespectful to our mother, the cook, and our father, the provider. The meal over, my older and middle brothers and I began clearing the table, hoping for a quick escape, when things took a sudden turn.

Charles Otis Ramsey, husband of Zannett Clopton Ramsey, father of Lester Stewart, Michal Ann, Ronald Otis, Douglas Wayne, and Kim Zannett, put on his white overalls and everybody ran for cover. The donning of the overalls was a clear warning: my father was about to fix something... badly.

The clues were there if you knew what to look for. My mother, who had several serious sewing projects underway, did not go to the sewing machine, but rather through the French doors leading from the dining room onto the sunporch. On her way, she picked up a brightly colored blouse she was making for my sister, with the intent of hand stitching white lace onto the peter pan collar. She also retrieved a flashlight from the top left drawer of the credenza.

Otis, as he was known by friends and family, was a man of many talents and much determination. But why he thought he was handy was, at the time, a mystery. All the hot and cold faucets in our house were reversed due to a day of plumbing on Daddy's part. The washing machine was held together with duct tape and would shock the shit out of you if wet hands touched metal. The fourth step on the stairs leading to the upstairs bedrooms gave a strange *crrrreeeek*. There was one small corner in the basement covered with wood-like paneling—the project started and never finished. And the list went on.

My dad usually started "fixin'" after dinner on his off days. You could tell that this was going to be a big fix by the number and kind of tools he brought up from his toolbox in the basement. In addition to the standbys, screwdrivers, pliers, monkey wrench, and hammer, his assault arsenal included electrical and duct tape, electrical wire, a hand drill, and an auger bit. An industrial strength flashlight, the kind that requires about 10 D batteries, completed the weaponry, and the battle began.

Hammer in hand, he walked up to the baseboard in the living room by the fireplace and hit it twice with a big ball peen hammer that my brothers and I nicknamed George. The plaster crumbled in defeat and a big gaping hole, about the size of shoe box, appeared. The six of us, my brothers, sister, and our dog, Skipper, escaped into the warm early evening air of the front porch to make plans.

It was decided to organize a baseball game with the neighborhood gang, and we headed for the park. What we called the park was actually an island that divided Second Street for about half a block, starting between Federal and Johnson Street. The space was lined with trees and, in the spring, covered with grass. But by late summer, thousands of steps by neighborhood kids running, jumping, and playing, stomped the grass into a hard, dirt-packed surface perfect for freeze tag, baseball, and hide-and-seek.

The thing that was so great about the park was that it was a neutral zone; everybody played, no matter size or age; everybody argued, about whose turn it was, or what the rules should be; everybody cheated, whenever the opportunity arose; everybody had a good time, screaming and yelling, laughing and joking.

The five Ramsey children ranged in age from 15 to two. My brother Lester being the oldest, my sister Kim being the youngest. My brothers Wayne and Ronald were four and eight, respectively, and I would be 12 in just a few months. We didn't usually play together—age and interests sent us in different directions. But on this occasion, we were united in our efforts to escape the fixin'.

"Baseball," my brother Les declared, and we headed for the park, Kim riding piggyback on her big brother, Wayne and Ronald each wearing cowboy hats, cap guns strapped securely to their waists, and me, braids flying, bangs standing straight up in the air, lifted by the cool evening breeze. Kids emerged from houses along the block: Arthur Braggs, known as Squealer, and his two younger sisters, Pat and Yvonne; Dennis Porter; Ronnie Farmer; Patsy Campbell. Bats, balls, and gloves were gathered and the game was on.

We played until dusk, and the one rule we all knew stopped the game and sent us all running: *Be home before the streetlights come on.* This rule didn't really apply to my brother Les, but he, too, joined the stampede.

As we headed toward 720, the signs were not good. The house was dark, which meant that our father was still working on the plug.

Once on the front porch, we could look through the screen door to see Daddy poring over the small booklet that came with the new outlet he was trying to install. The flashlight sat aimed at the page, his lips moving slightly as he carefully checked the next step in the process.

Daddy appeared and spoke through the screen door, his command addressed to Lester: "Go down to the basement and try the lights."

He handed him the flashlight and my brother made his way through the living room, the dining room where my mother still sat sewing, then through the kitchen and down into the basement. Nothing changed. My brother came up, my dad took the flashlight and fiddled some more. Down Lester went again, and again nothing happened. After two more attempts, our mother came to the front door, relieved us of the two youngest, Kim and Wayne, and took them upstairs for baths and pajamas. My father was, by now, mumbling and grunting to himself. I think profanity was part of this conversation with himself, but I couldn't quite make it out.

Les, Ronald, and I sat in darkness on the front porch eating apple fried pies. Normally, we were not allowed to eat anything other than popsicles or ice cream cones on the front porch, but this was not a normal night. The fried pies were one of my favorite desserts, and although my editors advised against including recipes in this writing, I am putting it in anyway.

My mother started the fried pies off with four cups of dried apples, gently simmered until soft in a cup of water seasoned with sugar, cinnamon, and nutmeg. Once the mixture softened, butter and vanilla flavor were added, turning it a rich, rusty-brown color. Kind of like apple sauce, but somehow much, much better.

While the apples cooked, Mama made the dough that would hold the filling. Flour, salt, Crisco shortening (always chilled), mixed together until crumbly. Icy cold water was added a few drops at a time until the ingredients came together to form a ball. Mom pressed a small round bowl down onto the surface of the rolled-out dough, creating four-inch circles. She filled each circle with the apple filling, carefully folded the dough over the mixture, and sealed it by pressing a fork around the edges. Each pie was gently laid into the big black cast iron frying pan, which held about a half inch of hot Crisco shortening. Browned on both sides, they were removed from the pan and sprinkled with cinnamon sugar, a job usually done by me.

Les, Ron, my mother, and I got two each, Kim and Wayne one, and my father got four. My brothers and I tried to steal each other's pies, hiding them from each other in spots around the kitchen. My mother often shared hers with the two younger ones. No one touched Daddy's fried pies.

He was eating one in the living room, flashlight going back and forth from the troubling outlet to the pamphlet. He made a few more adjustments and sent Les to the basement. The lights went on, then off, then on. We waited. They stayed on. Success...

of sorts. In the lamplight, Daddy inspected the outlet, grunted and walked away.

It was years later that I would come to understand that it was upside down. It was also a few years later that the house had to be totally rewired. The electrician said he was surprised that an electrical fire had not ignited and burned the house to the ground. The fixit fairy was clearly watching over my father... and the rest of us, as well.

Daddy had many friends. High lifers, movers, and shakers in the community and city, and low lifers, slinking around, up to no good. His friend, Mr. MacAdoo, was on the low end. He owned a small, mildly successful construction company, but had several other ventures that were to the left of being legal. My mother did not like him, and in hindsight, I could see why. MacAdoo was big, well over six-feet-five, tipping the scales past the 300 mark; Black—similar in color to Old Blue—and loud: talked loud, laughed loud, dressed loud. Whenever he and my father got together, there were usually shenanigans of some sort. Like the time the two of them drove up to my Aunt Laura's summer house in Idlewild to bring me home after a two-week visit.

On the way back to Saginaw, MacAdoo said to my father, "Otis, bet ya fifty dollars ya can't make it home in an hour."

The path from Idlewild to Saginaw was a two-hour trip down a two-lane road, which passed through several small towns—Baldwin, Clare, Reed City. Daddy didn't say a word, just smiled, squared his shoulders, squinted, and pushed the pedal to the medal. The big powder blue Oldsmobile 98 rose up, yelled *zoooooom*, and we rocketed down the road, hitting 100 miles per hour, flying through the small towns, never once slowing down, the two men laughing, passing back and forth a small paper cup filled with a golden-brown liquid.

I knew I should have been frightened, but truth be told, I was having a great time, windows down, the wind chased its tail round and round, lifting my bangs straight up and my two braids straight out. We flew past the Saginaw City limit sign 59 minutes later.

"Damn, Otis!" MacAdoo said. "That was somethin'!"

"Yep," Charles Otis replied, slowing down and holding out his hand for the $50.

Then there was the time Daddy and MacAdoo cemented over the side yard to create a driveway on the front side of our house. Mr. MacAdoo owned a small construction company housed on the old Bay City highway and had volunteered to help with the project. MacAdoo arrived in the early afternoon on a Wednesday, my father's half-day at the barber shop, driving an enormous truck with a cement mixer grinding and clanging away on the back. The two set to uprooting the flowers, shrubs, and grass, leveling the ground in preparation for the cement. It was hard, sweaty work on a hot summer day. Sitting on the front porch, with my legs dangling over the side, I was the gopher, bringing cold water, matches for cigarettes, the occasional cold beer. They laughed and joked, but there was quiet conversation, the kind you have with longtime friends who shared a common past.

"Hooowee!" MacAdoo said. "This is like being in the cotton fields back home in Alabama!"

"Naw," said my father. "There ain't nothin' harder than pickin' cotton. Sun up to sun down, bent over, head down. Row after row after row."

"Yea, ya right, Otis," said MacAdoo. "Hated that life. Tired, poor, barely makin' do. Run off soon as I could."

"Me too," said Daddy. "Took me a couple a tries, and I don't think Papa ever forgave me for it, but I just wanted a chance. I dint mind the work, I was a big strong kid, I minded the life."

"You go back home much?" MacAdoo asked.

"Last time was eight years ago when my Mama passed," my father said. "But I think about home. It wasn't all bad, ya know, runnin' and playin' in the woods, fried salt pork, fresh hot biscuits and syrup for breakfast, Papa sittin' on the porch smokin' that old corn cob pipe of his. I think that's why I took up the pipe, cuz it reminded me of him."

The cement mixer was turned on low, just enough to keep the mixture from setting up. The ground ready, MacAdoo cranked it up to high. The noise alerted the neighborhood, and kids joined me on the porch. Adults congregated on the sidewalk in front of the house. My mother came out onto the porch, took one look, shook her head, and retreated back inside. MacAdoo got into the driver's seat, backed the truck up into the side yard and pushed the lever, creating an opening in the bottom of the container. Wet cement slowly oozed onto the yard, filling the space with a dull grey oatmeal-ish mix. Daddy stood on the side of the truck where he made hand gestures for MacAdoo to help the load fall into place.

Things got a bit dicey when it came time to smooth the cement into place, because the two men were racing against the onslaught of dusk and darkness. Mr. MacAdoo brought out tools that looked like giant spatulas with long handles and he and Daddy worked away at it. They got all the way to the end of the new driveway before darkness set in.

Their plan was to get together on Sunday afternoon and add the mini-ramp that would gently slope downward from the berm into the street, allowing a smooth entry into the space. That Sunday never came, and for as long as we remained on Johnson Street, entry and exit into the driveway involved navigating the three-inch gap between driveway and street. A definite bump in the road.

My parents had a full social life that included clubs and organizations, home dance parties, poker parties, social galas (in our circle), and celebrity appearances at the Saginaw Armory, UAW #267 Hall, or the Saginaw IMA (Industrial Mutual Association). I had seen the home dance parties and poker parties from the inside, as my parents were often the hosts. The five of us were banished to the upstairs, but laying on our stomachs, peering through the bannister, we had a clear view of the living room.

Our mother passed through from bedroom to dining room. She carried her 40 years well, and looked glamorous to the five of us in a navy blue cap, sleeved dress flaring out from the belted waist with the help of the crinoline skirt underneath. Pearls and patent pumps completed the outfit.

Daddy strode by a bit later. Brown pinstripe suit, white shirt, dark brown patterned tie. His shiny reddish-brown gaiters walked gingerly across the carpeted living room floor, carrying feet tired from the long day at the barber shop. This was to be a poker party; my mother responsible for food, and soft drinks, my father booze and bar set-up. The finances they did together.

My father had stopped at several stores on his way home from work and his harvest included beer, scotch, bourbon, whiskey, gin, vodka, rum, cans of pineapple and orange juice, tonic water, bottles of coke, 7 Up, lemons, limes, and bags of ice. My father could make "tasty libations," as he called them, skills learned when he earned extra money as bartender at both the Saginaw Country Club and the Saginaw Club.

Daddy lined up the liquor on the dining room credenza, filled the ice buckets, put all the juices and soft drinks in a metal tub surrounding them with ice. A second tub was filled with ice and beer, the caps barely visible, looking like polka dots in the snow. Limes and lemons he cut into wedges and maraschino cherries swam in a small bowl of bright red liquid.

Charles Otis was also the banker at the poker table, so he carefully counted out coins and bills, checking twice to be sure of the starting amount. From the top drawer of the credenza, Daddy procured a thick padded cloth and a smooth tablecloth, spreading them out on the big dining room table. He laid six brand new decks of Bee playing cards—three red, three blue—on the table. All was ready.

Although friends often came to our house to socialize, listen to music, dance, eat, and drink, this evening was a different event.

This was a pay party. There was a charge for both food and drinks, and the house took a percentage of the gaming wins. But the music, dancing, and socializing were free, and a good time was had by all who came. The crowd would include mostly friends and neighbors, their husbands, wives, girlfriends, boyfriends, and some strangers looking for a game of chance. Our dining room table sat eight, including my father as banker, so seven played cards at a time.

Others sat around, ate, danced to the silky sounds of Billy Eckstine and Joe Williams, talked, and joked. Sometimes the records in the back of the TV console came out of hiding, and the comedy of Red Foxx, Moms Mabley, Pigmeat Markam, and Slappy White would set the house to chuckling. Much of the humor was off-color and not meant for children's ears. I think our parents knew we were listening, and probably only my older brother Les could really understand the humor, but the sound of laughter drifting upstairs made me know that downstairs was a happy place highlighted by the smell of chicken and fish cooked by our mother, the throw-back-your-head laughter of our father, the *whoop* of the winners, complaining of the losers.

To be clear, this was not the gambling big time. Most groups at the table bet nickels, dimes, and quarters, others bet in dollars, ones, fives, the occasional ten. A really big pot would have been perhaps $300, which was huge in 1958, when the average income was around $4,000 a year.

The night usually ended around 2:00 or 3:00 a.m., the five of us long gone to bed. Our parents would clean up and figure out their profit for the evening before turning in. Of course, the next morning, as soon as I saw my father, I would ask how much "we" made. And as usual, he never actually said.

"We did pretty good," was the stock answer.

Six days a week at the barber shop, weekend jobs as bartender, the occasional poker party. It all added up. We really did do pretty damn good.

Sometimes Otis would go out with some of the men from the party to one of the many after-hours joints peppered around the Black neighborhoods. These places opened for business around 2:00 a.m. when the bars closed. Some were in basements, others in backrooms of stores or restaurants. They were kind of like the poker parties, or maybe not. The place was not so clean, the food not nearly as good. The drinks were not so fancy, but cost twice as much, and the gambling was not nickels, dimes, and quarters, but rather fives, tens, twenties, and fifties. There were loan sharks and sporting women, factory workers, and businessmen.

A good time was had by all and the joints didn't close till the sun came up. These forays were not something I asked my father about, and what I am explaining here, I learned about much, much later in my life. What I did know was that my mother never went, and my father only went if the party at our house was very successful. And when he did go, Sunday definitely created a two-pajama day for him. The house and all in it quietly waited while he slept late, took naps, and read the paper.

My daughter Ashleigh, as a small child, looked at her father, my husband Rocky, as he came out of the bedroom dressed to go out to a dance for the evening.

"Dad," she said, "you look sturby."

Sturby thereafter became the word used in our family when someone was dressed up and looking good. My father often looked sturby. But never so much as when he and my mother were stepping out for the evening for one of the big dances sponsored by the Baker's Dozen Club, Frontiersmen Group, or some other organization. These functions were usually held at the big UAW Hall on Washington Street, big band sound provided by Estrom Broom and the Sweepers, and my parents danced and socialized with Black folks from all over the city. They were a good-looking couple, she fair and petite in a strapless ball gown, he tall, dark, and handsome in a black three-pieced pinstriped suit and black wingtips. They came home late, laughing and talking. In the morning, we would usually find swizzle sticks on the kitchen table for us. Red ones from the scotch and water on ice my father enjoyed, and blue ones from the iced Coca-Colas my mother drank.

The pace of summer flowed on with sunny days, playing outside, my mother canning fruits and vegetables for winter, my father running the barber shop. Our Chicago relatives usually came to visit early spring and late summer. My Uncle Elton, my mother's brother, came, bringing with him my father's half sister, Aunt Marie, and our cousin Martha, my father's other half sister, J.B.'s half sister. The visit was fast and fun. Martha went fishing, then made colored spaghetti. Marie made blackberry cobbler and sweet potato bread and cried with happiness and called the five of us her babies. My uncle brought a carton of cigarettes, scarves, and purses for my mother, straight off the back of the mysterious truck. They came and went with hugs and kisses, pats and love, and the house felt quiet and empty without them.

Elton

There was, however, a different kind of visit that started in 1956, the year my sister Kim was born. My Uncle Elton married Virgie Lee Walters, and the two began coming at the end of the summer for a week. The vibe was very different than the frenetic pace of Martha's, Marie's, and his two-day weekend whirlwind. They were on vacation.

Some years ago, one of my husband's many uncles passed away and at his funeral, the minister stood up took a deep breath, let it out, struggling for words that just would not come. Finally, he said simply:

"You all knew him."

And the congregation nodded and shook their heads. This was so the truth about my Uncle Elton. We all knew him, knew that he could in no way be described as an easy person to live with, deal with, and be around. He was prickly and quick tempered, took offense when none was intended, and never ever forgot what he considered to be a slight or snub.

All of these traits weighted the scale heavily in favor of someone you would not like, and there were many who took that route. That was not, however, the case in our house. With the quick temper came a quick wit, and a wonderful memory for dates, times, and places. He told a great story, and could tease you without malice into laughing at the things in life that tripped you up.

Like my brother Ronald, my uncle was a man of his word. If he said he would, he would without fail, and he expected the same of you. The other game changer about my uncle was his love and lifelong devotion to my mother. They were born 11 months apart in desperately poor, hard times in the backwoods of Louisiana. Their mother, my grandmother Eva, died when Elton was three days old, poisoned, it was said, by their father Willie Clopton's wife. They were raised by their grandmother, my great-grandmother. When they were 13 and 14, my great-grandmother died of cancer, and they went to live with their aunt, my great-aunt Sylvinie, known as Nanny. My mother spoke little of her early life, but my uncle, late in his life, could be coaxed into revelation.

"I loved my grandmother," he would say. "She made the best tea cookies you ever tasted, soft and sweet. She would put 'em high up on a shelf to keep me from 'em. Didn't work. I would stand on the kitchen counter, reach up onto that top cabinet and bring down the jar. Then, me and Tee would take a bunch, stuff them in our pockets, put the jar back, and run off into the woods and eat 'em. She did her best," he would say, shaking his head, conveying that it was just a tough time in a rough place.

"My uncles, Elton, Mac, and Floyd, was mean," Uncle Elton would explain. "They worked hard and played hard, drinkin', cursin', and fightin'. Weekends was the worst. Granny would tell me and Tee to hide. Sometimes we hid under the bed, sometimes just off the back porch, out of sight, out of mind. My Uncle Mac had a woman, and they would straight-up box. She would pick and pick and pick, hitting him and pushing him till he hauled off and knocked her out cold."

I listened intently as Uncle Elton continued.

"Me and Tee, we didn't let nobody mess with us. Now I would fight, but your mama, she was crazy fearless. She'd get a running start and jump you, fists flying, screaming, kicking, and scratching, till she took you down. I was the same about her. We couldn't catch a break. We was mixed race in Loozeana. Too light to be Black, too dark to be white. They called us names, picked and taunted. And we took on all comers."

His smile at the memory did not reach his eyes. "There ain't nothin' I wouldn't do for her, and I know she's the same about me."

My Uncle Elton was called by four names. He was always called Brother by my mother, father, and all adult relatives. In fact, I did not really know his name was Elton until I was about six. My brothers, sister, and I called him Uncle, just Uncle. His wife Virgie Lee always called him Clop.

Back in the day, Uncle was a "player." My mother and he shared the same cream-colored complexion and jet-black wavy hair. He was small of build, five-foot-five... on a good day, wiry and quick. Back in the day, he dressed the Chicago Gouster style: black pinstriped suits with oversized shoulder pads in the jacket, draped trousers cinched at the waist, caramel-colored cap, toed gaiters, crisp white shirt, snap-brimmed fedora. A gold chain looped from waist to knee. *Hotchacha!* He was good to look at and could charm you right out of your clothes, which he often did. He married his first wife, Mattie Lucille Evans in 1940, had two children, Gertha Lee in 1941 and Elton Evan in 1942.

And here is that "six degrees of separation" thing. My father had been friends with both Nanny and her common law husband, Charlie Hopper. My father married Nanny's niece, Zannett. Zannett's brother, my Uncle Elton, married Uncle Charlie's niece, Lucille.

It was not a happy match. He hated Aunt Lucille's mother, and it was mutual. When his son Elton was born, Lucille's mother made sure the boy was named Elton Evan Clopton, not Elton Clopton, Jr. Fifty years later, his anger about it was still a tangible thing that shimmered and glowed. Perhaps that is why he never liked his son. His daughter Gertha Lee fared no better.

I do not understand why he did not like his children, and it has always saddened me that it was so. For the five Ramsey children, he was the best of uncles. He encouraged us, seemed to genuinely like being around us.

When writing about my aunts and mother, I said that there were things that I knew that you did not need to know about. This is true of both my father and my uncle, and this is what I am willing to share about my uncle.

He and Lucille divorced in 1950. I was four and have little to no memory of Aunt Lucille. They had been separated for many years before the divorce, during which time he had a long-term relationship with Irma, who was quite a bit older than him. It was a rocky, stormy relationship and Irma left him and moved out to California to live with one of her grown daughters. While she was gone, Uncle met and married Virgie Lee Walters in 1956. That was a shock to Irma, and she hot-footed it to Chicago, determined to get Uncle back. Although she never actually got him back, there was a "byside" relationship (a side-chick in today's parlance, one step below a mistress) for a few years before Aunt Virgie found out and delivered the ultimatum.

This story cannot go forward without talking about my Aunt Virgie. In many ways, she was so not like my mother and my other aunts. In a time when women stayed home, had children, kept house and cooked, my Aunt Virgie did none of that. Born and raised in Jackson, Mississippi, she had gone to college and gotten a degree in accounting. In 1945, she and her childhood friend Rose moved to Washington to work for the War Department. At war's end, they moved to Chicago. Rose married and had two children. Virgie moved in with the family and got a job working in the accounting department for the University of Illinois. It was a happy, successful living arrangement and she was considered a member of the family, a much-loved Aunt to Rose's two children.

She dressed in two-piece suits with peplum jackets from Carson's Department Store in the Chicago Loop, wore peep-toed pumps and wonderful colorful hats. She couldn't cook worth a damn and was a so-so housekeeper. But she had the sweetest, kindest nature, and could talk to and warm the heart of a stone. She had a wide-eyed innocence about her, even though she was in her late thirties, often missed the punchline in jokes, and could be talked into believing the most unlikely things.

We first met Aunt Virgie in 1956, the year they married and my sister was born. On their first drive to Saginaw from Chicago, Uncle convinced her that there was an old, rickety bridge that had to be crossed just before getting to Saginaw. He made it sound scary and dangerous and had her on the lookout all the way until they pulled into our driveway. So, my first memory of her was a beautiful woman laughing full-body style, shoulders shaking, face scrunched up, eyes shut. She came in, pinched our cheeks, pulled us in for hugs and pats. The love between her and my uncle was a living, breathing thing. It would be so for 50 years.

Have I mentioned that, like my father, my uncle was a barber? Yep, he was. He finished Barber College not long after Daddy. Once his apprenticeship was finished, he started up his own business, and owned and operated several different shops on Chicago's South Side.

I spent a good amount of time in his shops during my summers there, and was familiar with the sights and smells of the tonsorial parlor. It was very much like my father's barber shop, but there were subtle differences. There were more white shirts and ties than blue collared work wear, more posturing and bragging, and an edgy big-city tension that I never felt in Saginaw.

My first cousin Elton shined shoes in the shop on the weekends, and when I was visiting, he and I would sit together on the sidelines, watching and listening. My cousin got paid 25 cents a shine, and each time a customer flipped him a quarter, he would give me a nickel for keeping him company.

Like my father, my uncle did not allow profanity, or what they referred to as "lowlife talkin'." They were both great storytellers, but my uncle's style was the gotcha, the comeback, the put-down. One of my favorites was the story about "The Big Shot." He told it often, but I guess it was my favorite because I was there when it happened.

"This ole guy," Uncle would begin, "came struttin' in ta the shop one Saturday afternoon all puffed up and important. Everything he had on was shiny. Shiny black three-piece suit with a shiny gold watch peekin' out the vest pocket, white shirt with a gold collar pin, and shiny diamond-studded gold cufflinks at his wrists. Liked his shoes though," he'd say with a knowing smile. "Black Stacy Adams wing tips. You remember him, Michal Ann," he'd say, giving me a wink.

"Yes, sir, I do," I'd reply with a smile.

"I knew he was shady the minute he opened his mouth," Uncle would continue. "Looked like he was talkin' out the side of his neck." Uncle would tilt his head to the left, quirk his mouth to the right, and assume the voice of James Cagney in *Top of the World*. "Started everything he said with well, er, ah, and don'tcha know. Well, er, ah, how long I gotta wait for a haircut? I'm a important man, got things ta do." Uncle narrowed his eyes, a sign most of us in the shop knew would not bode well for the shiny man.

"There's three ahead of ya," Uncle answered. "Unless someone's willing ta let ya go ahead of 'em."

Uncle looked up; everyone else looked down. Silence. Carefully the man took off his jacket, hung it on a hook, then took a handkerchief from his back pocket and wiped off the seat before sitting. My uncle's eyes were now slits. It seemed as though he slowed down his movements, intent, I now understand, on making the man wait longer. Conversation picked up and flowed around the room—talk of baseball, politics, crime. The voice of shiny Jimmy Cagney could be heard above it all, constantly interrupting to correct and postulate.

"Well, er, ah, the Cubs didn't actually beat the Sox, them guys cheated. Don'tcha know, you gotta have money like me to have a house on the lake. I put in a offer on one last week," he lied.

Finally, when the man was in the chair, my uncle asked him what he did for a living.

"Well, er, ah, I, uh, do many things, sell real estate, own a couple stores on the East Side, bout to close a deal on a building not far from here."

"Oh yeah," Uncle answered, and I could see the wheels turning. "What kinda stores?"

"Uh, you know, clothing, furniture, stuff like that," came the answer.

Uncle slowed his clippers, and gently turned the chair so the man looked out at the rest of us, but could not see Uncle. Heads perked up and conversation slowed. He winked at his audience and commenced the rapid-fire probing.

"New clothing or used?"

"Well, er, uh, some new, some not so new."

"What about the furniture, that not so new, too?"

"Well, er, uh..."

"So," Uncle interrupted, "you got a used furniture and clothing store. Where 'xactly is this store, I might wanna go there. What's the address?" Uncle was beginning to smile.

The man was starting to look uncomfortable and, in an effort to change the conversation, he snapped his fingers and called my cousin over to shine his shoes. Cousin Elton quick-stepped across the room and sat down on a low stool in front of the man and propped his foot up on the shoeshine stand. That's when we saw it, the hole in the bottom of his shoe. Not just a little spot, but a hole as big as a silver dollar, which meant it had been there a good while.

My cousin Elton bent to his task, grinning like a Cheshire. He knew what was coming. My Uncle Elton behind the chair had yet to spot it and the questioning continued.

"So, now where is yo' store?"

"Well, er, uh, it's kinda on the corner of Halsted and Court."

"Kinda, what's that mean, it's either on the corner or it ain't."

"Well, uh, er, uh, I'm kinda in a temporary place right now," he mumbled.

"You mean like a truck or somethin' like that?" Uncle said with a chuckle. "That's all I ever seen on that corner. So, if it's temporary, where you moving to?"

"Well, uh, you see, uh, uh, I'm gonna be moving my businesses up to Wisconsin."

I was nine years old at the time, old enough to recognize lying, and this man was so bad at it. My uncle kept up the questions, and the man with all the shiny baubles seemed to lose his huff and puff, while steadily digging a hole of untruths. It was soon clear that he did not have what he said he had, did not do what he said he did, and was not who he was pretending so hard to be.

Uncle walked slowly around the chair, checking the haircut for symmetry and anything he missed. When he and the man came face to face, Cousin Elton stepped back and discretely pointed to the hole. Uncle Elton's face said, "Gotcha!"

My Uncle made a big production of whipping the cape off the man's front, dusting him down with talcum powder, even helping him on with his jacket.

"Well, uh, ya know hotshot," my uncle said in a dead-on imitation of the man, "I, er, uh, know you're a busy man and all, but you might wanna make a stop at the shoe repair and get that big hole in them fancy shoes fixed."

The barber shop roared with laughter and the man beat a hasty retreat out the door and disappeared into the flow of people on the busy street.

One of the customers spoke up, "Aw, man," he said to Uncle, "You shouldn'a embarrassed that guy like that."

"Maybe not," Uncle replied. "But he started it with all that lyin' and pretending. All kinds'a folks come through here, doctors, lawyers, day workers, bus drivers, thieves, cops, whatever. I don't care who they are or what they do, I give 'em respect. Haircut, shave, mustache, trim, what they ask for. We chat a bit, they pay their money and go on their way. But you come in my place talking stuff and holding court, I'm gonna take you down a peg. Count on it."

At the time, I saw the humor in it, but felt badly for the man and the circumstance he must have been in. My uncle, however, had no remorse, and told the story many times with great relish and much laughter.

I thought this story would not be about food and cooking on 720 Johnson Street, but here it is again. You see, although my Aunt Virgie did not cook, my uncle did, and it tasted just like my mother's. My father rarely rattled the pots and pans, but he had a specialty... pancakes. So, on the Saturday and Sunday during their visit, Uncle made smothered spareribs, and Daddy made pancakes.

It started when my mother, my aunt, and I left the house Saturday morning and headed downtown. Our first stop was Baisley's Meat Market. Among the regular weekly purchases were added two slabs of pork spareribs, carefully trimmed, tops cut off and cut into tips. My part of the shopping was over and I was dispatched to 720 carrying two shopping bags, hamburger, neck bones, round steak, bacon, liver, sausages, and the ribs, each wrapped in white butcher paper and secured with twine. My mother and aunt stepped away in the other direction, laughing and talking.

Straight home, through the house and into the kitchen I went. My father, taking a rare day off, and Uncle sat at the table talking quietly. Daddy slowly puffing on the pipe he always filled with cherry wood tobacco, Uncle taking long pulls on a Lucky Strike. I started putting the meat into the refrigerator, but sat the ribs on the kitchen counter. Uncle immediately got up and set to work. My father's role in all of this was somewhat like Aunt Virgie's; he participated in the conversation, but not the work. He remained relaxed and comfortable sitting at the table, the sweet smell of smoked cherries wafting from his pipe.

I guess you could call me the sous-chef, pulling things from the fridge, finding pots and pans and other utensils in a kitchen that Uncle was very comfortable in, but not totally familiar with. And as always, I listened. They were talking politics.

Standing at the sink, head bent, he gently rubbed as water sluiced over the ribs.

"It's gonna happen," he said. "No matter what they do to try and stop it. Like one of them hurricanes we get down home, whipping up a frenzy, whirlin' and turnin', changin' everything."

My father nodded in agreement, smoke from his pipe swirling around his head.

The "it" my uncle was referring to was equal rights. The eye of that storm was 1958. Dr. Martin Luther King, Jr. had become a force to be reckoned with, having successfully led boycotts and sit-ins and marches across the South, preaching peaceful resistance and iron resolve. I understood well racial prejudice because I lived it, the snubs and slights, places we as children knew not to go, lines that could not be crossed. My uncle was right; it was going to happen.

There was a quiet time in the kitchen, my father's cherrywood tobacco mixing with the smell of frying pork and browning rue.

"I'm glad our boys are too young to go to war," my father said, his breath disturbing the smoke swirling about his face.

"Me too," my uncle agreed. He added water to the rue, making the *swooshie* sound I knew well. He covered the pot, lowered the fire to a click and sat down at the table.

"You know," he said with a humorless smile, "it ain't really a war, it's called the Viet Nam conflict."

"I don't care what you call it," Daddy replied. "American boys are going over there and coming back in boxes. I was in World War Two. I know what a hell hole it can be."

My uncle smiled again; this time you could see the twinkle.

"You know, Otis, they almost had me, but I slipped through their fingers. I was down at Fort Leonard Wood, Missouri, training for the infantry. I didn't like it one bit. Someone telling you what to do and when to do it... when to eat, when to sleep, when to dress, hell, when to shit. Always yelling, nothing ever good enough, lousy food. So, I decided I had had enough and I was gonna leave. So late that night, I sneaked out the gate, just walked away. Hoboed my way back to Chicago and never looked back."

He laughed at the memory. My father did not, the hard set of his mouth clearly announcing his disapproval.

The two men sat across from each other, both looking out at the pleasant sunny day. Inside our kitchen, however, there seemed to be a big thundercloud encircling the elephant that sat between the two. I found myself holding my breath.

The front screen door banged open and light came into the house. Zannett, loved by Charles Otis and Elton, and Virgie, adored by her husband, my uncle. Arms full of packages, faces full of happy. The kitchen seemed to relax into the place I knew and loved.

I don't know that the Fort Leonard Wood story was truth, or just another over-the-top tale told by my uncle. I do know that, although nothing was said out loud, it made my father angry and my uncle repentant. I never heard mention of it again.

I was old enough to finish dinner: canned corn and rice. I started cooking when I was nine and my mother had been ordered by Dr. Claytor to be on bed rest as much as possible. She would tell me what to do in the kitchen, step-by-step, from bed. I would hustle into the kitchen, do that, bring the pot to my mother who would look and smell, tell me if something needed to be added, then send me back for the next step. Unlikely as all of that seemed, it was a system that worked.

The adults ate dinner in the dining room, Uncle tenderly teasing Aunt Virgie, my mother laughing and joking right back. The kids in the kitchen were having our own fun: the three older ones, Lester, Ronald and myself, sharing things our parents did not need to hear; Kim in the highchair, obliviously stuffing meat and rice into her face; and like my father, my brother Wayne sat quietly taking it all in.

Sunday morning, a quiet house, Mama still in bed and Daddy in the kitchen. Only one possibility here. My father was making pancakes. Hot damn! Charles Otis Ramsey made the best pancakes ever, ever, ever. Light, fluffy, golden brown, smelling of butter and vanilla, they filled your mouth with deliciousness.

There were problems with Daddy's wonder pancakes: one, he produced enough batter to feed thousands. He said he learned the recipe in the Navy and that's how he made 'em. The idea of dividing things in halves, thirds, or fourths was not on his radar. He dealt in bowlfuls, gallons, and dozens.

The second problem was that in the making, he used every bowl, pan, and spoon in the kitchen. Flour was everywhere, including on Daddy's clothes, the floor, the table, and the stove. Sugar spilled out of the bag, eggshells rolled around the tabletop, bumping into boxes of soda, bottles of vanilla. There was going to be a lot of cleanup.

When my father was wearing his white fix-it coveralls, we scattered, leaves in the wind, hoping not to be asked to help. But the pancakes, that was different. Our baby sat in the highchair. We four sat at the kitchen table, hands in our laps, because there was no place on the table for them to go. It was mesmerizing. The dry ingredients in a big giant bowl, Daddy adding one slightly beaten egg at a time, beating each one in a separate cup or saucer, butter melted on the stove, waiting to be added.

The best part of the whole thing was that my father talked the whole time. Had he been alone, he would have been mumbling to himself, but with his children as audience, he went full-on monologue. He talked about the Navy:

"The first time we sailed out of the harbor, I cried like a baby, 'fraid I wasn't gonna get back home, but I did and now here I am with you."

We'd all laugh because *you* was his first name for all of us: "You Lester, you Ronnie, you Michal Ann." The *you* and our name was usually followed by a command.

Now adding the melted butter to the mix, stirring, tasting, he continued:

"I didn't like it, I was a cook, all the coloreds were. That put us in the bottom of the ship." Reaching into the fridge for a small-canned container of orange juice, he opened and poured. "The sound of them bombs made yer head pound and yer heart take off racing. We was in the bottom of the boat, and if somethin' happened, we was dead, plain and simple."

We sat silently staring at our father.

He must have realized that he should not keep going with this. Adding about a half-gallon of milk to the bowl, he picked it up, tucked it under his arm, and started slowly mixing.

"Did I ever tell you how I met yer mama?" he asked, a grin forming, head slightly tilted, eyes stopping on each one of us. Yes, we knew, but, "No," we answered in unison.

"Well," he said picking up the pace of the spoon, creating a soft *plt, plt, plt.* "I was playing on a baseball team down by Opelousas. I was a damn good player, but I was all the time breaking somethin'. Both my ankles, my arm, my wrist. They called me Bones back then, cuz my bones was just so brittle. Anyways, once I seen her out the corner of my eye, I couldn't stop peeking atter. She was the prettiest thing I ever saw, tiny, not even a hunderd pounds, a Creole with smooth creamy skin and jet-black wavy hair."

Lighting the stove to heat the griddle, he went on, "So, I'm pitching, really bad, the other team scoring, cuz I'm looking at yer mama and throwing the ball straight at the batter. I look at her and she's looking right straight at me, smiling. Next thing I knew, the ball hit her right upside the head, BAM and down she went."

By now, we had all put our elbows on the flour-covered table, hands on either side of the head.

Dropping batter onto griddle, he turned back to us.

"Hell, I thought I'd kilt her. There was a ruckus, people crowding around to see if she was okay. It took a few minutes, but she pulled herself up on her elbows, looked straight at me with that same smile and says, 'Ya know, Otis, you ain't no kinda pitcher.' She was it for me. And ya know what I got?" He asked.

"I got you," he said, looking at us. "And a whole lot more."

The griddle produced three pancakes at a time, so when he got five, we dug in. There was no bacon or sausage, just pancakes and Alaga syrup. All you needed. He kept the griddle going and started a pot of coffee. My mother arrived, said hello, and he gave her a pancake covered with syrup. She took her coffee and pancakes into the dining room. My uncle and aunt came in last, no longer able to resist the smell of pancakes and caffeine. My uncle was used to this, but this was my Aunt Virgie's first experience and her face was priceless.

What she saw were four children, arms covered in flour and other unidentifiable things, sitting at a table full of everything: cups, bowls, bags of sugar and flour, cutlery beaters, and eggshells, a toddler happily rubbing syrup on her face, and about 100 pancakes piled up on a platter on the stove.

"Boo," my uncle said, patting his wife on the shoulder. "Get yer pancakes and come on into the dining room."

Daddy served himself last and went to join the adults. We were in no hurry, there was no escape, we would be cleaning up.

Breakfast finished, Uncle and Aunt Virgie made ready for the trip back to Chicago. They departed the same way they arrived, hugs and kisses, pats and rubs. My mother took my sister Kim upstairs for a bath. My father sat in the living room with pipe and paper, and we headed to the kitchen to wash and scrub, wipe, and put away. My brother Ronald hated kitchen duty more than the rest of us and had the annoying habit of stuffing pots, pans, and dishes in the stove, like that would make them disappear. They never did.

Our mother came back into the kitchen, releasing us from duty. (Ronald would be recalled about the stuff in the oven.) Daddy was no longer in the living room. He had gone upstairs for a bath. He would come back down in pajamas and robe ready for a nap.

It was Sunday at home, 720 Johnson Street.

Epilogue

My Parents

When I look at pictures taken of my father through the years, he always looks as though someone yelled, "Attention!!!" Shoulders back, standing tall, staring at the camera. But if you look closer, you will see the glint in his eye, the slight upturn of his mouth, hinting at a smile.

Daddy was our provider and I think the work ethic all five of us developed was due to his example. He started out working the logging camps in Texas and Mississippi, came North for the factory work, went to Barber College at night, and eventually owned both Cantu's Barber Shop and The Ramsey Market next door. No small feat for a man with barely a grade school education.

My father lost both of his legs in the early 1970s, the result of hardening of the arteries. With the aid of prosthesis, he continued to be amazingly self-sufficient, cutting hair for a few long-time customers, driving to the store to play his lottery numbers. Ten years older than Zannett, he survived her by three years.

My mother, Zannett Clopton Ramsey, was not one who went to the doctor. Seventeen years after my sister was born, my mother's friend Elizabeth bullied her into seeing a doctor. She died four years later of complications from primary pulmonary hypertension. She was 62. If that sounds harsh, the reality of that was much worse and my heart still breaks at the memory. But that was more than 40 years ago.

I am healthy, fit and strong, already 12 years older than her at her end. I know that in many ways I am like her—soft spoken, iron-willed, family first. But I am also very different. I don't suffer life stoically. I proclaim, loud and often, my love, my hopes, dreams, my anger. And I know without a doubt that I was her favorite. My sister and brothers thought the same thing. They were wrong.

My Siblings

It was said that Kim Zannett Ramsey Young looked like my father's youngest sister Carrie, who looked like Aunt Marie. She quickly left behind the Winston Churchill look I described earlier. Like Aunt Marie, she grew up to be an imposing woman, big, tall, and beautiful, with our mother's jet-black wavy hair and our father's smooth dark complexion. She had the artist's touch and created big bold canvases full of life and color. She had two sons, Elton and Michael. They have grown to be good, kind, loving men: Elton calm and laid back, Mikey quick and loquacious.

In her early thirties, Kim began an incredible religious journey and the Lord's call was for her loud and clear. She became an ordained minister and eventually bishop in her church. Our paths diverged for a while and we were estranged, but we found our way back to each other. When she was diagnosed with pancreatic cancer some years back, I was with her every day of her final journey.

Douglas Wayne Ramsey grew to be a very big man, six-five, 300-plus pounds. He was a star athlete in high school, and although he finished but one year of college, he was one of the smartest people I knew. A voracious reader with a quick wit and wry sense of humor, he and I had great debates about authors, stories, and characters from shared novels. My brother was an amazing baker, and although his lemon pound cake was a thing of beauty, it was his peach cobbler hot out of the oven that made you want to stand in the pan with a spoon and eat your way out.

Wayne was quiet and soft-spoken, and people often associated that with a lack of intelligence. A huge mistake. My baby brother fought and won the battle with the drug addiction of his youth and held on to sobriety for more than 30 years. He had one son, Jason Z. (The initial a nod to his grandmother), who looks a lot like him and has his same quick wit and gotcha sense of humor. Jason has four children: Jay'la, Jason, Janae, and Jayden Wayne.

My brother died at 53 of complications from Hepatitis C, before Jaden was born. We recently came across a picture of Wayne as a child of three. The sweet face smiling out at you from the photo looks exactly like Jayden. That seems only fitting.

Ronald Otis Ramsey rarely left Saginaw. It was where he wanted to be, felt he had no need to venture far from home. He seemed to remember everyone he ever met, all the way back to his kindergarten days at Crary Lincoln Elementary School, and friendships formed as a child remained strong throughout his lifetime. My brother would tell you that he was not well-read, but he could quote statistics from basketball games played 20 years earlier, knew what football players were traded where and when, and who won playoffs, Super Bowls, and World Series last year and the year before. He smoked Kool cigarettes, played the lottery, and ate everything fried and greasy or swimming in gravy.

Ronald was truly a family man and, although he had no children of his own, he was devoted to his nephews—Elton Wayne,

Jason Z, and Michael Kai—and had a soft spot in his heart for my daughter Ashleigh Zannett. He could be grumpy and blustery and a bit of a bully, but it is a case of the bark and the bite, and no one could deny that was steadfast and true, a man of honor. If he said he would, he would and expected nothing less from you.

Ronald and I were close. We talked on the phone almost daily and he came often to dinner. Ronald got sick in 2012, and illness took him down a 10-year path of hospitals, doctors, medications, and pain. He fought back and held on, but when the pandemic came in 2020, he just had nothing left to fight with. It has been five months. I am wounded.

Lester Stewart Ramsey left Saginaw more than 50 years ago, as the song says, "Looking for adventure!" If there was a picture in the dictionary to accompany the definition of risk taker, my brother would be staring out at you. He is a world traveler, having spent time in Africa and Asia, and now lives in Amsterdam and New York. He speaks fluent Dutch, can converse in French and Spanish, and has the annoying habit of being able to correct your grammar with the pluperfect form of a word. (Who does that!)

My brother had the remarkably good fortune to have found, 40 odd years ago, his partner in life, my beloved "outlaw," Lammert deJong. Their homes have been a haven for me, a place where I am welcomed, loved, nurtured, and refreshed. Lester is one of my best friends, someone I can talk to about all things, and count on anytime, always. We two are the last of the seven. We hold the keys that unlock laughter, love, joy, sorrow—the memories of home. So, brother, remember always 720 Johnson Street and the smell of lilacs.

The Relatives

Martha Gregory lived for more than 100 years, feisty and sharp of mind to the end. After her husband Greg's death, she moved to a small apartment near Wrigley Field in Chicago, but spent a large part of her time in Greensburg, where she had a small trailer. Some years before her death, my brother Les spent time with her at a family reunion in Gulf Shores, Alabama. She made colored spaghetti. He said it was good. I bet it was.

Marie Armstead moved back to Saginaw in the early 1970s. She had a small house a block-and-a-half from our house. She stayed until 1979 when she moved to Hammond, Louisiana, where the warmer weather was much better for her arthritis. I spent several summers there with her. Her last visit to Saginaw was in 1986, when she came for the birth of my daughter, Ashleigh Zannett.

My husband Rocky, our daughter, and I spent a week with her in Hammond in 1988, and one of our most treasured photos is of her, my daughter, and me smiling happily out at the camera. It was a sweet visit. Auntie sat most evenings in her big armchair with the brown paper bag nearby. We watched Cubs games on TV, she held

Ashleigh on her lap, and taught Rocky how to eat crawfish. "God don't like ugly," but He surely loved my Aunt Marie.

Laura Dudley Bristol had a summer house in Idlewild, Michigan for many years. Her original intent in building the house was that it would be a good place for my older brother to go in the summer and get relief from his asthma. The reverse was true and Les was never able to be there more than a few days without experiencing severe asthma attacks. She and Uncle O.B. lived there year-round for several years before moving to Saginaw to be closer to my mother when her health began to fail.

Urban Renewal replaced Nanny's neighborhood with the Dan Ryan Expressway. With her children grown and on their own, she moved to a small apartment; Uncle Charlie moved nearby. I visited her many times when I was a student at Western Michigan University. I loved listening to her tell tales of naughty deeds done by my mother and uncle, how beautiful my grandmother was, and the fun the two of them had when they went "out steppin'." Most visits, she sent for a big bag of greasy fried shrimp and, of course, a Diet Rite Cola to wash it all down.

My Uncle Elton and Aunt Virgie moved from Chicago to Saginaw in the 1990s to be closer to family. We saw them almost daily, shared food, celebrated birthdays and holidays. The two of them did everything together, cooking, shopping, taking short trips back to Chicago. Alzheimer's was prominent in Aunt Virgie's family and she, too, slowly drifted into that twilight space. My uncle was bereft.

About the Author

A friend of mine, having read a rough draft of this story, said I should add in more stuff about myself. I tried, and it sounded like an Oscar Night acceptance speech. I am educated, with a B.A. and an M.A., and I had a 35-year career in education, teaching a range spanning second grade to graduate college levels.

I have travelled: Africa, Europe, the Caribbean, most of the 50 states.

But I am most proud that I have family and really good friends, the kind that show up and stand up. A sweet, patient, kind, loving man who is my husband and partner of more than 50 years; a treasured daughter who calls me just because; the five of us, the aunts, great aunts, cousins, nephews, and on it goes.

Bless your hearts, for you have surely blessed mine.

The Recipes

Nope. I am not writing out the recipes. Although there is a lot of cooking here, this is not a cookbook. All of the ingredients are given, and how you put them together is explained. But these were people who cooked in pinches, dabs, and pours, and if you don't know what you are doing, you should not be fooling about trying to make these dishes. But go ahead, try them.

Lightning Source UK Ltd.
Milton Keynes UK
UKHW010638090522
402703UK00001B/10